FRESH IDEAS IN
découpage

Colette George

NORTH
L GHT
BOOKS

NORTH LIGHT BOOKS

CINCINNATI, OH

WWW.ARTISTSNETWORK.COM

745.546

about the author

PHOTO BY MICHELLE ALAIMO

Fresh Ideas in Découpage. Copyright © 2005 by Colette George. Manufactured in China. All rights reserved. The patterns and drawings in the book are for personal use of the reader. By permission of the author and publisher, they may be either hand-traced or photocopied to make single copies, but under no circumstances may they be resold or republished. It it permissible to make the projects contained herein and sell them at fairs, bazaars and craft shows. No other part of this book may be reproduced in any form or by any electronic or mechanical means including information storage and retrieval systems without permission in writing from the publisher, except by a reviewer, who may quote a brief passage in review. Published by North Light Books, an imprint of F+W Publications, Inc., 4700 East Galbraith Road, Cincinnati, Ohio, 45236. (800) 289-0963. First Edition.

09 08 07 06 05   5 4 3 2 1

Distributed in Canada by Fraser Direct
100 Armstrong Avenue
Georgetown, ON, Canada L7G 5S4
Tel: (905) 877-4411

Distributed in the U.K. and Europe by David & Charles
Brunel House, Newton Abbot, Devon, TQ12 4PU, England
Tel: (+44) 1626 323200, Fax: (+44) 1626 323319
Email: mail@davidandcharles.co.uk

Distributed in Australia by Capricorn Link
P.O. Box 704, S. Windsor, NSW 2756 Australia
Tel: (02) 4577-3555

George, Colette
  Fresh ideas in découpage / by Colette George.—1st ed.
     p. cm.
  Includes index.
  ISBN 1-58180-655-8 (paperback: alk. paper)
  1. Decoupage. I. Title.
  TT870.G4 2005
  745.54'6—dc22
                    2004030216

Editors: Jessica Gordon, Tonia Davenport
Designer: Karla Baker
Layout Artist: Donna Cozatchy
Production Coordinator: Robin Richie
Photographers: Christine Polomsky, Al Parrish
Photo Stylist: Jan Nickum

Throughout her successful design career, Colette George's creations have always reflected her reverence for nature, her passion for new ideas and her organic and spontaneous approach to art. She credits her identity as a designer in large part to her father, who fostered in her a love of design and experimentation.

This extraordinarily creative artist has earned a reputation for design excellence throughout the state of Oregon and has recently received enthusiastic national attention as well. With an extensive background in many facets of retail design and display for public, private and corporate sectors, Colette is being offered many publishing and communication opportunities showcasing her work. In addition, she has recently signed with Susan Osborne Licensing, Inc. (see Resources, page 126).

Colette would like to take this moment to acknowledge her husband, Ted, whose support and sacrifice have at times been nothing less than breathtaking. They live together with Bruce Springsteen in a beautiful little town called Riddle, Oregon.

To find out more about Colette and her work, visit her website at www.colettedesigns.net.

METRIC CONVERSION CHART

To convert	to	multiply by
Inches	Centimeters	2.54
Centimeters	Inches	0.4
Feet	Centimeters	30.5
Centimeters	Feet	0.03
Yards	Meters	0.9
Meters	Yards	1.1
Sq. Inches	Sq. Centimeters	6.45
Sq. Centimeters	Sq. Inches	0.16
Sq. Feet	Sq. Meters	0.09
Sq. Meters	Sq. Feet	10.8
Sq. Yards	Sq. Meters	0.8
Sq. Meters	Sq. Yards	1.2
Pounds	Kilograms	0.45
Kilograms	Pounds	2.2
Ounces	Grams	28.3
Grams	Ounces	0.035

dedication

To my sons, Austin and Ty: In an effort to inspire you to pursue your dreams, you've inspired me to pursue my own. I dedicate this book to you.

acknowledgments

I am privileged to have this opportunity to publicly thank the people whose support and faith have not only contributed significantly to CGDesigns but also to the edification of my soul. Without their recent, past, and often continual support, my voice would never have been heard.

Sincere thanks to Larry and Carol Linten, Linda Johnson, Bonnie Gregory, Teresa Houde, Diane Hand, Judy Cuthbertson and Marolyn McCullough for their practical, heartwarming support and refusal to give me blank stares, although it's easy to imagine they were tempted.

Thank you to these esteemed folks for their warm support and encouragement: Gary and Janice Quist and the helpful, kind crew at Roseburg Book and Stationery; Marilyn Home & Garden; Rose Cottage Studios; Sandra Beckwith; Dori Koberstein and Karen of Anna Christina's; Garden Gate Nursery and Florist; and thanks also to Ruth Botens; Mary Ann Winters of Wintergreen Nursery & Florist; and Julie Schenck.

A very special thank you to Kay Peterson of Reed & Cross for artful friendship, graceful inspiration and commercial advice to Off the Streets. Many of you had no idea the timing was so critical! We are indebted to you all.

I am also grateful to Tricia Waddell for being curious about my work and asking me to write this book, and to the whole team at F+W, whose confidence contributed greatly to my freedom. Thank you also to Ann Porter O'Brien, Patrick and Cassandra Millsap, Diane from Peachy Blossoms, and Kathryn Simon of Common Folk Company for the unexpected generosity! A hearty thank you to Javelin, Laurette, Julia and Bob, and my friends at SCD.

Warm thanks to Barbara Brown, Sondra Erbe and Linda Ely for their belief in my individual creative ability at important crossroads. Hugs to Lynette Covert for sharing business, friendship and dark humor (what a relief), and also for introducing me to my agent. To my agent, Susan Osborne, I so appreciate your patience while this book was being created.

And...thank you to my closest friends: Cindy Buchheit, Lauren James Berlingeri, Debbie Matthew, Betti Manfre, Joy Morin (friend and photographer! check out the Summer Snaps project, page 26), Barbara Kilkenny and new friend Tonia Davenport. Our divinely coincidental lives have left me no choice but to have hope for tomorrow and peace for the day.

My life and art have been enriched far beyond measure through my friendships with all of you. I'm honored and thrilled to be a part, large or small, of all of your lives.

contents

introduction

Having worked as an interior decorator and as a stylist in home décor stores for many years, I have a great interest in decorative home accessories of all styles. I love browsing through home décor and antique stores, flea markets and art fairs to find unique objects that will be the perfect piece for a home or a store display. Sometimes, of course, I don't find exactly what I'm looking for, but I always go home with something equally valuable—inspiration for handcrafting an accessory that is infused with my personal style.

Fresh Ideas in Découpage focuses on helping you to create decorative accessories using current retail home décor items as the standard and inspiration. I will give you techniques you can use to skillfully blur the line between handmade and professionally manufactured, showing you how to achieve the layered and textured detail of the sophisticated pieces sold in your favorite home décor shops. The collage concept is currently exerting a great influence in the home décor realm, and this book puts you on the cutting edge of that trend.

If you're picking up this book, you already know how satisfying it is to create a piece of personalized artwork, developing it from idea to finished product. Look through your and your family members' attics and scrapbooks to find ephemera (vintage paper items), and make photocopies of them to use as personal artwork in your découpage projects. Celebrate the history of your family, a special achievement or event by incorporating these tokens of the past into your present decorating scheme. For many of the projects in this book, including the Retro Runner (page 56) and the Garden of My Youth specimen box (page 68), I have incorporated photographs and mementos from my past.

In addition to the personal items you use in your découpage projects, just look to the wonderful selection of papers now available. I marvel at the incredibly beautiful artwork found on paper today. Readily available papers create exciting opportunities for crafting lovely home décor accessories with ease. The explosion of scrapbooking and papercrafting has generated abundant style choices with such affordability—most papers cost literally pennies. The projects in this book use reproductions of illustrious artwork in common forms such as napkins and tissues (available from most drugstores). Sources of these estimable images include the Metropolitan Museum of Art New York (Pour Toi Tin, page 96) and the Victoria and Albert Museum of London (Wall Cone, page 82). A wide selection of images is also available through clipart books.

In addition to being affordable and available in a huge selection, paper images can also be easily altered. You'll learn many simple aging techniques that make paper elements as well as ribbons take on a vintage look, as in the S'Mores House Call Toolbox Kit (page 60) and the Romantic Letter Box (page 86). And you'll learn how to layer paint, wax, plaster, stain and even ink to create elegant finished pieces. You'll also learn how to choose the best kinds of papers, and how to tear or cut them in a certain way to add to the overall effect of any project.

Many of the projects showcased in this book are from very successful lines produced by my company (like the Bird Canvas [page 40] and the Eiffel Tower Wall Hanging [page 102]), and they reflect some of the most vastly popular décor styles being implemented in homes today. You'll enjoy each section—Modern Country, Nature, Retro, Romantic Cottage, Old World French and Zen—and you'll draw inspiration from each unique style.

basic materials

PAINTS, STAINS AND SPRAYS

Adding color, shine and aged effects to your découpage artwork gives your pieces personality, dimension and interest. Use the following paints, stains and sprays to create and maintain your projects.

ACRYLIC PAINTS are craft paints that come in every color and finish imaginable. They are easy to mix and thin when you want to achieve different results.

METALLIC FINGER POT RUBS are metallic waxy rubs applied with the fingertips that are traditionally used to highlight relief areas, such as on frames. They are available in bright colors as well as in "metal" colors, including gold, copper and silver.

OIL STAIN is an oil-based pigment traditionally used to protect and color wood. I use it to make letters stamped in wax stand out from their plain background and to add an aged effect.

ANTIQUING MEDIUM is a type of craft paint specifically used to create an aged look. I use Apple Butter Brown by Plaid when using wax and other aging techniques.

CRACKLE SPRAY PAINTS (I use Make It Crackle! by Krylon) are layered over each other to create a crackly, aged surface. Step 1, the basecoat color, is applied first. When it has dried, Step 2 (usually in a contrasting color) is sprayed over it. A reaction with the first layer produces fissures in the top coat of paint so that the basecoat color is visible through the cracks.

ADHESIVE SPRAY (I use Super 77 by 3M) is a multi-purpose adhesive spray that makes it easy to apply adhesive quickly to a large surface area.

CLEAR LACQUER SPRAY (I use Preserve It! by Krylon) is an aerosol spray that helps to keep inks from running when used with water-based glues.

PRESERVATIVE SPRAY (I use Make It Last! by Krylon) is a vital aerosol spray that prevents crackle paint from flaking.

FROM LEFT TO RIGHT: DÉCOUPAGE MEDIUM, SUPER 77 SPRAY ADHESIVE, MAKE IT CRACKLE! STEP 1 & STEP 2, WATER-BASED GLUE, WEBBING SPRAY AND CLEAR GEL TACKY GLUE. IN FRONT: DECKLE-EDGE SCISSORS AND PRE-PRIMED CANVAS.

PAPER, SCISSORS AND GLUE

When creating collage art, quality papers, scissors and glue are essential. Today, there is an endless variety of papers—they come in designs ranging from map reproductions to depictions of aged surfaces; of scissors—there are about as many deckle-edge pairs as there are days in a year; and of glue—there are kinds that dry matte, cloudy, shiny and even glittery.

PRE-PRIMED CANVAS (I use Fredrix canvases) is a surface prepared especially for paints. It is sold on stretcher frames, in yardage, sheets, and also in placemat and coaster sets.

MULBERRY PAPER is a semi-transparent paper with a fibrous texture that appears delicate but is actually quite strong.

SCRAPBOOK PAPER comes in all weights (cardstock, text-weight and vellum). Take your pick from an inexhaustible variety of prints and designs.

DECKLE-EDGE SCISSORS are scissors that create a decorative edge as they cut. The particular set used for the Retro Runner project (page 56) replicates the vintage edge of old photos. Many other edge shapes are available.

A CRAFT KNIFE has a razor-like blade attached to a narrow shaft for easy control. It is used to make precision cuts.

DÉCOUPAGE MEDIUM is a thick, spreadable glue that dries clear or cloudy with either a matte or a shiny finish.

WATER-BASED GLUE is a white glue that can be easily thinned by adding a little water.

MISCELLANEOUS MATERIALS

In my découpage projects, I like to mix a variety of mediums and materials to create unique effects. You'll need a few basic materials—including beeswax and joint compound—to create these layered and textured effects.

BRISTLE BRUSHES are paintbrushes with synthetic or natural bristles. You'll use one with paint or hot wax to create texture. Inexpensive brushes work great for most projects in this book.

FOAM BRUSHES are paintbrushes made of a dense gray foam that creates a solid, smooth coat of paint.

STENCIL OR POUNCE BRUSHES are round, thick bristle brushes used for applying paint at a 90-degree angle to the surface, so that no bristles are forced under stencil edges.

JOINT COMPOUND is a thick white or off-white substance similar to plaster. Joint compound is inexpensive and comes in small quantities. It's sold in all building supply centers.

BEESWAX is untreated wax (like that used for making candles) available in convenient one-ounce bars, bleached or unbleached. Unbleached bars can vary in intensity of yellow.

QUILTING PINS are straight pins with large, multi-colored heads, used in the Garden of My Youth project, page 68.

ORRISROOT GRANULES act as a holding agent for fragrance oils. They are available by the ounce at most natural food stores.

SAND-BLASTING SAND is normal sand mixed with very fine particles of glass. It is used in the projects in this book to add extra shine.

FROM LEFT TO RIGHT: BRISTLE BRUSHES, GLUEPOT WITH BARS OF UNBLEACHED BEESWAX, STENCIL BRUSH AND FOAM BRUSH.

MISCELLANEOUS TOOLS

Most of the projects in this book are very simply constructed, and a handful of them require some basic and easy-to-find tools that you probably already have on hand.

NEEDLE-NOSE PLIERS are long, tapered pliers used for bending and shaping wire.

AN EYELET SETTER AND PUNCH is a pencil-shaped metal hole-punching tool with interchangeable tips used for making holes in any kind of material, or in a spot that cannot be reached with a hand-held punch.

A DRILL/SCREW GUN is an electric tool with interchangeable tips used to drill holes or drive screws into wood.

A LEVEL is a useful tool for making sure that all of the elements in a project are straight and/or flush.

AN OLD BUTTER KNIFE or a similar dull, flat-edged instrument is used to spread on joint compound.

basic techniques

CRACKLE PAINT

Before applying crackle paint to your actual project, practice on a scrap of cardboard to get the feel of the technique. It's a very easy technique, especially once you get the hang of it. And if you don't like what your first attempt produces, you can always start over. Just be aware that the surface texture will change as more layers are added.

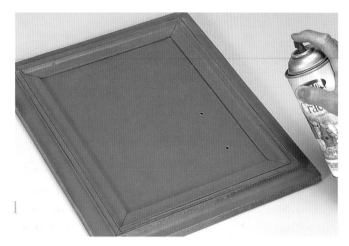

BASECOAT WITH CRACKLE

Using the can marked "Make It Crackle! Step 1," spray the object with an even coat of paint in a sweeping motion to create a solid covering. Let dry.

SPRAY WITH CRACKLE

With the same sweeping motion, spray "Make It Crackle! Step 2" on top of your basecoat, avoiding any runs and covering it in an even layer. The thicker the layer of Step 2, the more pronounced the crackle effect will be. However, be careful to apply the paint in one continuous layer, without letting it dry.

APPLYING WAX

Melted wax adds great texture and interest to découpage artwork. Use a gluepot to heat up the wax, and apply the wax to your piece with a bristle brush.

HEAT WAX & BRUSH ON

Set a block of beeswax in a gluepot with a temperature regulator and heat it to about 195°F. Beeswax boils when it reaches temperatures greater than 199°F, so adjust the heat frequently, keeping it between approximately 190°F and 199°F. Dip an inexpensive bristle brush into the melted wax and brush it onto your surface. The cooler the wax, the more the bristle strokes will show, which is often a desirable effect. Don't use your brush again for anything else—simply leave it in the wax, and the beeswax will melt away from it the next time you use it.

APPLYING JOINT COMPOUND

Joint compound has the consistency of mud, and it's easy to spread and layer. Depending on how thickly it's applied and on the climate of your work area, it can dry relatively quickly. I speed up the drying process by laying finished pieces behind a wood stove.

APPLY JOINT COMPOUND TO SURFACE

Begin with a butter knife or similar tool and load your blade with joint compound. Holding your canvas or base at an angle, lay your knife on its edge and slide the compound off a little at a time onto random areas—don't cover the entire surface. Turn the empty knife on its side and level out high places. Leave tiny dots of compound on the images, but don't cover up significant detail.

FINISH PIECE WITH JOINT COMPOUND

When layering wax, stain and joint compound, it's often a good idea to smooth on a final layer of joint compound to create dramatic texture. Apply joint compound sparingly over the layers of wax and stain with a knife to finish.

DRYBRUSHING

Drybrushing is a great way to add color without completely covering up the surface you're working on. It works very well on surfaces like galvanized tin and wood.

TEARING IMAGES FROM PAPER

Tearing images from paper is fairly easy, especially when you know what you're looking for. Pay close attention to how you rip around the images you choose—it can influence the way your entire project turns out.

Dip your bristle brush into the paint and wipe off all excess paint until the brush is almost dry. Drag your brush across the surface, pressing into the surface a bit if necessary.

Buy the best artwork you can find, and then locate good breaking points in the design, leaving images whole as you tear. Determine your base color to help you decide what can be omitted. Always rip in irregular shapes (no straight lines), and leave margins when desired. Try to keep focal points intact.

modern country

Modern Country style is an implied way of life—it's casual and celebratory,
reflecting the sensibility of the awaited weekend. The Summer Snaps project
(page 26) in this section reflects this celebration in a casual seasonal display.
In Walk Along the Oregon Coast (page 32), the use of memorabilia recreates
the joy of a beach gathering with a vintage touch.

Modern Country is also about a clean look in surface finishes, and it's
about minimizing clutter. In the Pear Pail project (page 14), the finish of
galvanized tin brings a shiny surface to the country home that has, for many
years, utilized primarily rustic matte surfaces. European country stylings
strongly influence the Modern Country home, and the Pear Pail uses a typical palette of an Old World European-style pear image and couples it with
bright galvanized tin. Pulling green and purple from the image helps to
blend the colors of the pears with the shiny silver and is also an example of a
popular color combination often found in design today. Modern Country,
adhering to its rustic roots, continues to incorporate aged surfaces, but in
fresh and clean new ways. In addition to mixing tin and Old World images
and palettes, well-loved American country themes are mixed with the aged
surface created by crackle paints, as in the Chicken Cabinet Panel project in
this section (page 22).

pear pail

A vast array of images is now within reach for découpage artists. With the wide diversity of scrapbook papers, beautiful napkins, tissue wrap and wrapping paper available, the crafting world has received an infusion of unprecedented size. Many clipart books and CDs have also been created, producing a proliferation of sources for clipart. I took the image for this project from Dover Publications, and there are other great sources of quality images available as well, such as the artwork from The Vintage Workshop (see additional artwork, page 124).

MATERIALS AND TOOLS

- galvanized pail (8 quart)
- pear images enlarged to 175% (Dover Old Time Fruits and Flowers Vignettes)
- classic alphabet stamps (All Night Media)
- black inkpad
- Lavender acrylic paint (DecoArt Americana)
- Hauser Light Green acrylic paint (DecoArt Americana)
- Bittersweet Chocolate acrylic paint (DecoArt Americana)

- bristle brushes
- adhesive remover (for removing labels)
- water-based glue
- Matte Preserve It! spray (Krylon)
- vinegar
- paper towels
- scissors
- craft knife
- cutting mat

from one artist to another

To help center the word and the image on the pail, use the handles as a visual guide. Simply adhere your images at the midpoint between the handles on both sides.

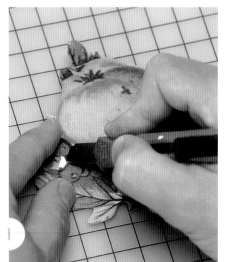

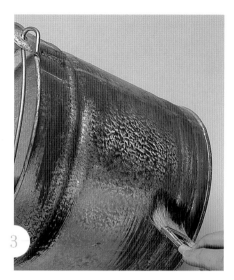

1. **CUT OUT PEARS**

    Make two pear clipart enlargements and cut
    them out with scissors. Cut around detailed
    areas with a craft knife.

2. **PREPARE PEAR IMAGES AND PAIL**

    Spray the cut-out pears with the Preserve It!
    spray and set them aside to dry. Using vinegar
    on paper towels, remove all of the oily and
    adhesive residue from the pail.

3. **DRYBRUSH PAIL WITH LAVENDER**

    Dip a dry bristle brush into the lavender paint
    and blot off the excess paint on a paper towel.
    Begin drybrushing the paint onto the pail (see
    Basic Techniques, page 11). Brush color hori-
    zontally down the seam to highlight it, and also
    apply paint to all of the raised crease areas.
    Leave areas bare in the center of the front and
    back of the pail and in other random areas.

4. **DRYBRUSH PAIL WITH GREEN**

    Randomly fill in areas over and around the
    lavender with the light green, using another
    dry brush. Make sure that the galvanized fin-
    ish continues to show through the paint.

5. **STAMP WORD ON PAIL**

    Using the alphabet stamps and the black
    inkpad, stamp the word "PEARS" at the top of
    the pail on the front and the back. (Letters can
    be stamped lightly and do not need to be too
    terribly straight.) Spray the stamped letters
    lightly with Preserve It! spray.

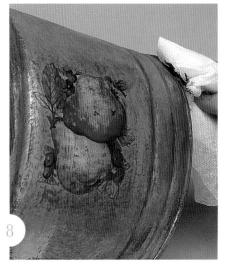

6.

ADHERE PEARS TO PAIL

Using a clean bristle brush, spread glue over the back of one pear image. Center the pear horizontally and vertically below the stamped word on the front of the pail. Smooth it down well and make sure all of the edges adhere to the pail. Repeat with the remaining pear image on the back of the pail.

7.

BLEND IN PEAR IMAGES

Spread just a slight amount of Lavender paint across the front of each pear for added interest and to blend the image into the pail. At the edges of the images, brush lightly away from the pears.

8.

HIGHLIGHT PAIL RIMS

Use a paper towel to add a bit of the Bittersweet Chocolate paint around the top and bottom rims of the pail. (Clean up around the rim if necessary.)

put your pails to work

BUCKETS HUNG IN UNIFIED ROWS FROM HOOKS AT ENTRANCE POINTS INTO THE HOME MAKE ATTRACTIVE AND CONVENIENT GLOVE AND HAT KEEPERS. JUST GRAB AND GO.

Sunflower Feeder

Use the same techniques as for the Pear Pail, but apply your chosen image to a galvanized tin feeder of any size. Using the Latin name of a plant is a great way to lend another layer of interest to your pieces. To find other botanical names for common plants, visit www.ernstseed.com (see Inspiring Websites, page 125). While traditionally used as a corn, grain or birdseed dispenser to be placed in the garden, you can also use the Sunflower Feeder to provide party sustenance. Simply fill it with M&Ms or another type of candy, and place it in a spot where your guests will feel free to dip in.

apple fiber pot

fruitful *frut-fəl adj* yield-ing or producing fruit, con-ducive to an abundant yield; abundantly productive

These fiber pots were originally designed in a voluntary effort to provide employment for my disabled sister, who was facing homelessness at the time. As a result of her hard work and our collaboration, several designs were created, and a little manufacturing company aptly named Off the Streets was born. It was a remarkable feeling to be able to pass along so many positive comments made by strangers to my sister about her work. Now she enjoys a productive lifestyle and is a volunteer herself! These pots sold very well, and it is with pleasure that I share this project with you for your own use or reproduction.

MATERIALS AND TOOLS

- no. 7 fiber pot, available in most flower shops (Recreations)
- apple-print napkin(s) (Caspari)
- water-based glue, thinned
- bristle brush
- paper towel

from one artist to another

THIN PAPERS SUCH AS NAPKINS, PRINTED TISSUES OR UNCOATED TISSUE WRAP (WITH NO SHINY FINISH) WORK BEST FOR THIS PROJECT. THEY ALLOW THE IMAGE TO MELD INTO THE SURFACE OF THE PULP POT SO IT ALMOST APPEARS PAINTED ON. WHEN CHOOSING YOUR IMAGE, MAKE SURE TO MATCH THE PAPER TO YOUR BASE COLOR AS CLOSELY AS POSSIBLE SO THE IMAGE BLENDS SEAMLESSLY INTO THE BACKGROUND.

THERE IS A PROLIFERATION OF BEAUTIFUL NAPKINS AND LIGHTWEIGHT TISSUES COMMONLY AVAILABLE IN DRUGSTORES AND HOME DÉCOR AND GIFT SHOPS. IMAGES FROM THE METROPOLITAN MUSEUM OF ART AND OTHER COLLECTIONS ARE REPRODUCED BEAUTIFULLY ONTO THESE PAPERS, PROVIDING A QUALITY AND SELECTION OF ARTWORK THAT IS SIMPLY STUNNING.

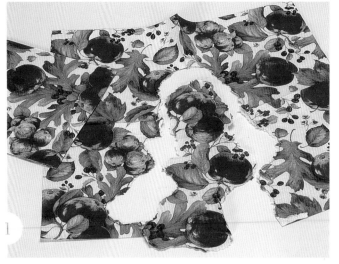

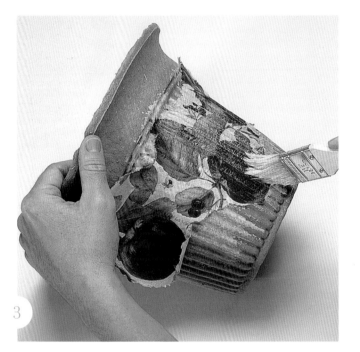

1. **TEAR OUT APPLE IMAGES**
   Open up the napkin and look at the apple
   images. Decide what elements need to remain
   intact, and rip them out of the napkin. The
   torn-out images should ultimately form a garland around the whole pot. Leave green at each
   edge, if possible. Moisten your fingers and roll
   away one ply from the back of each image.

2. **APPLY GLUE TO BODY OF POT**
   Make a mixture of the glue and water, using
   about one part water to two parts glue. Use a
   bristle brush to apply glue to the areas of the
   pot that will be covered by the image. Work the
   brush into each groove in the pot.

3. **ADHERE IMAGES TO POT**
   Lay the first image on the pot, positioning it so
   that part of the image goes over the lower por-
   tion of the top rim. Work the brush over the
   image, smoothing the napkin into the grooves.
   Begin in the center of the image and work your
   way to the outside, being careful not to stretch
   or tear the napkin.

handy tip

IF YOU ACCIDENTALLY RIP PART OF THE
IMAGE BECAUSE IT STICKS TO YOUR FIN-
GERS, PATCH IT WITH ANOTHER SMALL
PIECE AND MORE GLUE. SIMPLY APPLY A
LITTLE MORE GLUE TO THE POT AND FIT THE
NEW PIECE INTO THE SPOT. OF COURSE, YOU
MAY DECIDE TO LEAVE A HOLE OR TWO TO
ADD A WORN ASPECT TO YOUR DESIGN.

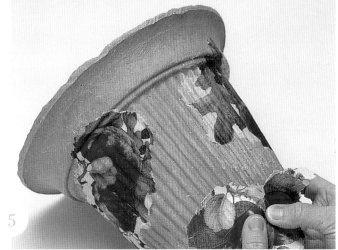

4.

5.

4. WIPE OFF EXCESS GLUE
While the glue surrounding the images is still wet, wipe off any excess with a dampened paper towel.

5. ADHERE REMAINING IMAGES
Lay out the other pieces to see how they will fit on the pot. Then add the rest of the images, creating a pleasing composition around the pot. If necessary, tear the last piece down to fit the space.

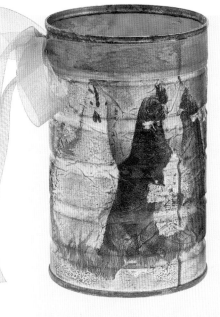

more on fiber pots...

These fiber pots are watertight, even when housing water for weeks. They come in varying sizes and dimensions and in three different colors: Basil, Bark and Straw. They are colored by actual straw, basil or bark fragments residing in the pulp.

In addition to being very durable, these fiber pots are also versatile. With grape images applied they make the perfect containers for chilling wines. Our customers have also used them as holiday centerpieces holding small evergreen or feather trees, or as gift baskets. Others use the pots as vases, filling them with fresh-cut flowers. As you begin this project, decide how you would like to use your fiber pot, and pick images accordingly.

Fiber Pots and Tin Can Luminaries
You may use the same concept as used in the fiber pots to create découpaged luminaries. I chose to use empty chicken soup cans for this project— with all of their nostalgic implications, they seemed the perfect choice. To make the luminaries, you can randomly drill holes in a clean tin can, then add images as desired. Then drybrush the cans with antiquing medium and rub a little black finger pot rub around the rim. To finish, place a candle inside the tin and tie a ribbon around the rim. It's best to use a tea light since tin can get so hot. Also, make sure to place the luminary on a protective dish.

chicken cabinet panel

crackle \kra-kǝl\ *n* a network of fine cracks on an otherwise smooth surface

The crackle effects used in this project imply age and are useful in Modern Country décor as well as in Old World stylings. This project shows you how to transform old and even somewhat damaged cabinet panels easily and quickly with user-friendly Make It Crackle! spray paints from Krylon. This technique is recommended for cabinets with a dull or porous finish for nice paint adhesion. Use good interior housepaint for the trim and existing stationary cabinetry. Where we will use black to add crispness and heft, you may instead match the paint to your chosen basecoat color for less contrast. With a larger central image, this technique may also be used on a single cabinet panel for wall décor.

MATERIALS AND TOOLS

- cabinet door(s)
- door hardware
- "Regal Rooster" rub-on transfers (Tulip)
- Make It Crackle! Step 1, Spanish Moss (Krylon)
- Make It Crackle! Step 2, Buttercup (Krylon)
- black interior paint
- metallic finger pot rubs (dark blue and black)
- Make It Last! clear spray (Krylon)
- sandpaper (optional)
- no. 8 flat brush (Royal soft grip)
- disposable bowl (for paint)
- scissors
- latex gloves

from one artist **to another**

SOMETIMES COMING UP WITH THE CORRECT PLACEMENT AND DISTRIBUTION FOR YOUR ART CAN BE TRICKY. WHEN DECORATING ALL OF THE CABINETS IN A KITCHEN, I RECOMMEND CREATING A FOCAL POINT ON PROMINENT PANELS AND ADDING ACCENTS (AT CORNERS OR ALONG SIDES) ON OTHERS TO AVOID A CLUTTERED LOOK.

ALSO, WHEN CHOOSING COLORS AND IMAGES FOR THE CABINET PANELS, CONSIDER THE VIEW FROM OTHER ROOMS.

1. **SPRAY CABINET WITH STEP 1**
   Remove the cabinet to be reworked from its hinges. If necessary, sand the cabinet lightly. Spray the cabinet with Step 1 of the crackle process, Spanish Moss (see Basic Techniques, page 10). The basecoat should provide nice, even coverage—avoid runs, but it's ok if the paint runs a little. Let it dry.

2. **SPRAY CABINET WITH STEP 2**
   Paint the cabinet with Step 2 of the crackle process, Buttercup. Apply the spray paint in an even layer across the panel, especially around the edges of the panel where the crackle effect should be most prominent. Apply the paint liberally, but avoid runs—a thicker coat of Step 2 makes bigger crackles. Be careful not to apply the Step 2 paint in layers, however, as you'll have to start over with Step 1 if multiple coats are applied over a dried layer of Step 2 paint. (Practice on a piece of cardboard first to get the hang of it.) Let dry.

3. **PAINT CABINET EDGE BLACK**
   Spray the entire cabinet with Make It Last! clear spray. Using the black paint and the no. 8 brush, paint around the outside of the cabinet. Run the brush flat inside the channel to get a nice, clean line without using tape.

4. **CUT OUT AND PLACE RUB-ONS**
   Loosely cut out the rub-ons you wish to use. Lay them out on the painted cabinet panel for placement. Set the handle on the cabinet for visual aid. Ideally, the bottom image should not go below the bottom of the handle.

5

6

5. ADHERE CHICKEN IMAGES

Remove the protective Mylar backing from the cut-out chicken rub-ons, and set the rub-ons in their spots on the cabinet panel. Start in the center of the first rub-on, and using the craft stick that came in the package, burnish over the entire image, going in both directions a few times. Be careful not to accidentally slip the stick under the decal. Remove the film from the top of the image and repeat for the other images.

6. ADD METALLIC FINGER POT RUBS

Choose metallic finger pot rub colors that coordinate with the rooster image, and randomly rub color around the frame of the cabinet with your finger. (Here I am using blue and black.) Set a piece of scrap paper over the images, and spray Make It Last! on the perimeter of the cabinet over the metallic finger pot rubs. Set the panel aside to dry thoroughly before adding hardware.

Floral Cabinet Panel

Using text on cabinetry contemporizes the design. In this piece, coordinating the color of the text with the crackle color created the first aspect of blend. Bringing in other colors and adding finger rubs in those colors brought another level of blend to create depth and interest.

To make this panel, choose images from floral tissue wrap and scrapbook paper. Apply slightly thinned water-based glue to the cabinet with a paintbrush, and smooth the floral images onto the panel. Do not use excessive glue, and avoid saturating the applied paper. To add whimsy and a personal touch, use something unusual for the pulls, such as an old silver serving spoon or a harmonica. Simply drill through the panel and the object to attach the handle, and add matching touch-up paint to the screws.

summer snaps

simplify \sim-plə-fī *v.t.* **to reduce to basic essentials**

When creating spontaneous temporary displays, you can let your imagination run free. There is no fear of commitment here—these displays are meant to be a celebration of the moment. This project is fast, fun and easily adapted to other themes, such as a Christmas or Valentine's display. Simply scatter loose snow and pine cones or confetti and candy hearts at the base of the display, depending on the theme. There are no rules for this project either. In fact, many of the materials used come from hardware stores. As a child, I would tag along with my father to hardware stores, and when I started to really look around, I was surprised at how inspiring all of the materials were. I drew on that experience to find this scupper drop and chef's hat pipe strainer, which are from the gutter or roofing section of the hardware store.

MATERIALS AND TOOLS

- 3" × 7" (8cm × 18cm) scupper drop (from the gutter or roofing section of a hardware store)
- chef's hat pipe strainer, 3" (8cm) (gutter guard)
- sandy beach scrapbook paper—1 sheet
- vintage-style black-and-natural grid paper—1 sheet
- black-and-white photos and/or old postcards
- natural reindeer moss (see Resources, page 126)
- sea grass or onion grass
- various shells, mini seashells, seahorses, sand dollars and sea glass
- one large starfish
- sand to sprinkle

- additional beach mementos (optional)
- manila tag (optional, for writing descriptive date and/or details)
- miniature clothespins
- washed gravel
- semi-flat black spray paint (Krylon)
- rubber bands or floral tape
- glue stick
- hot glue gun and glue sticks
- double-stick tape
- craft knife
- cutting mat
- scissors
- pencil

from one artist to another

THIS PIECE IS DESIGNED AS AN "ALL-AROUND" DISPLAY, MEANING THAT IT SHOULD BE VISUALLY APPEALING FROM EVERY VANTAGE POINT, LIKE A FLORAL CENTERPIECE. YOU MAY CREATE THIS ALL-AROUND PERSPECTIVE BY DIVIDING THE PIECE INTO THIRDS OR FOURTHS AND MAKING SURE THAT THE DESIGN ELEMENTS ARE EVENLY DISTRIBUTED AROUND THE PIECE.

ALSO PAY ATTENTION TO THE BACKS OF PHOTOS AND HOW THEY WILL BE SEEN FROM OTHER SIDES. LEAN PHOTOS IN A TIPPED FASHION AGAINST THE TUBE ALL AROUND THE BASE OF THE PIECE.

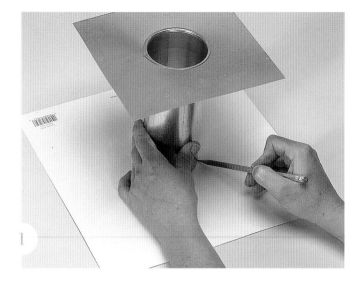

1. **TRACE AROUND SCUPPER DROP**
Center the shaft of the scupper drop over the sandy beach paper and trace around it with a pencil.

2. **BEGIN TO CUT OUT CIRCLE**
Slice an "X" in the center of the circle shape with the craft knife.

3. **COVER SCUPPER DROP SHAFT**
Measure the height and circumference of the scupper drop shaft, and cut a piece of the grid-style paper to that size to wrap around it. For the 3" × 7" (8cm × 18cm) scupper drop, the paper should be 7" × 9" (18cm × 23cm). Apply a line of glue with the glue stick to the seam of the shaft. Adhere one end of the paper, wrap it around the shaft, and apply a second line of glue to seal the other end of the paper.

4. **COVER BASE OF SCUPPER DROP**
Use the scissors to finish cutting out the circle. Don't worry about making the shape perfect, just make sure it's big enough to fit over the shaft. Place the paper over the shaft, right-side-up, then flip the scupper drop over and wrap the overlapping paper under the bottom of the flat base. Secure all four sides with double-stick tape placed under and near the edges of the base.

5. **PAINT CHEF'S HAT AND STARFISH**
Spray the chef's hat with two to three coats of the black spray paint. Let dry between coats. Spray the starfish as well.

6. **MAKE BUNDLES OF SEA GRASS**
Start with five to six strands of sea grass and wrap the ends together with floral tape, stretching the tape as you roll the bunch of grass to create tackiness that will help the tape adhere to the grass. Or, secure the grass with a rubber band. Make a total of about five clusters and set them aside for later.

7

8

9

7. **GLUE ON MOSS**
Glue clumps of the natural reindeer moss around the base of the scupper drop with the glue gun.

8. **INSERT SEA GRASS**
Insert the dry painted chef's hat into the shaft of the scupper drop. Slide the sea grass clusters down into the shaft, spacing them evenly between the spokes of the chef's hat.

9. **GLUE ON SEASHELLS AND STARFISH**
Using the glue gun, glue tiny shells or starfish into open areas on the black-and-white photos to accent them.

shoebox art

CASUAL LIFESTYLES ENCOURAGE A CASUAL APPROACH TO DISPLAYING PHOTOS. DIG INTO OLD SHOEBOXES AND COME UP WITH PICTURES, POSTCARDS AND MEMENTOS TO USE AS DECORATIONS. JUST CHOOSE PHOTOS AND EPHEMERA ACCORDING TO THEME, AND THEN LOOK AROUND AND ASK YOURSELF HOW YOU CAN INCORPORATE WHAT YOU'VE FOUND INTO YOUR DÉCOR.

FOR EXAMPLE, YOU MIGHT INSERT BLACK-AND-WHITE PHOTOS OF FRIENDS AND FAMILY WHO ARE MUSICIANS INTO THE STRINGS OF AN OLD GUITAR, AND THEN HANG THE GUITAR VERTICALLY ON A NARROW WALL.

OR CREATE A "MOM'S KITCHEN" OR "BAKING" SCENE INSIDE A DOMED GLASS CAKE DISH. PLACE A SHORT STRAND OF CHRISTMAS LIGHTS UNDER THE DOME AND MIX IN OBJECTS WITH DIFFERENT TEXTURES—OLD BUTTONS, OLD PHOTOS, FABRIC AND EPHEMERA.

FOR A TATTERED VIGNETTE, AGE CLOTHESPINS WITH RANDOM STAIN SWIPES AND THEN CLIP SEPIA-TONE PHOTOS TO FEATHER TREES OR STRUNG METAL CABLE. ADD ACORNS, PINE CONES, TATTERED RIBBON AND BITS OF WAXED BROWN OR BLACK STRING TO TIE DIMENSIONAL MEMORABILIA IN THE SAME COLOR PALETTE TO THE DISPLAY.

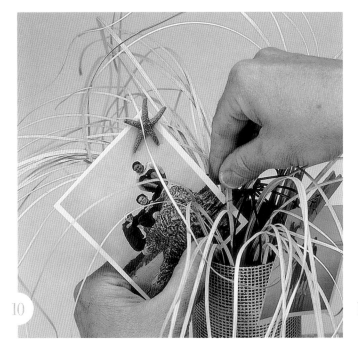

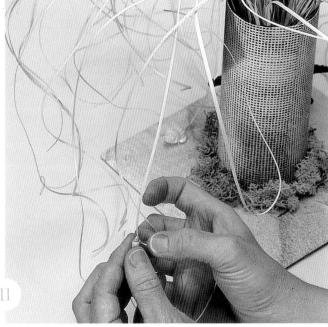

10. CLIP ON PHOTOS

Randomly clip the photos onto the chef's hat with the mini clothespins. You can also clip on postcards, if desired.

11. GLUE SEASHELLS ONTO SEA GRASS

Glue some of the tiny shells onto the strands of grass, using the glue gun. Again, placement should be random and at different heights. Use a total of about six or seven shells. Remember to include some at the back as well.

12. ARRANGE PIECE FOR DISPLAY

Set the finished piece where you wish to display it and randomly place mementos, additional photos, postcards and shells around the base, letting them spill out onto the table-top surface. Sprinkle the gravel around the base of the arrangement. Sprinkle sand around the base to finish.

walk along *the* oregon coast

Of course, it's possible that the most meaningful element to add to a piece of découpage artwork is words. Being a lover of books has kindled in me a love of text for its own visual beauty, and I love adding words and letters in any language to my artwork. Letters and words are never satisfied, always imploring you to stop, read and savor. Coupling ephemera with text creates a magical feeling that is unique to each design and designer.

MATERIALS AND TOOLS

- 8" (20cm) terra cotta bulb pot
- coastal news clippings (mine are from an old newspaper)
- postcards and photos
- beach-tumbled brick pieces or rocks, shells and moss
- twine
- scented sand
- 3 votive candles
- 3 votive holders (clear glass and/or mini terra cotta pots)
- white acrylic paint
- aged gold finger pot rubs
- water-based glue
- clear sealer
- Make It Acid-Free! spray (Krylon)
- bristle brush
- clear contact or matte laminating sheets
- scrap newspaper or bubble wrap (to create false bottom)
- packing tape (to tape over hole in bottom of pot)
- scissors

handy tip

WHEN DESIGNERS TALK ABOUT AN "A" SHAPE, THEY SIMPLY MEAN THAT ITEMS ARE LOOSELY ARRANGED ALONG THE LINES OF AN IMAGINARY LETTER A. YOU MAY CHOOSE TO ARRANGE THE ITEMS IN YOUR DISPLAY ANY WAY YOU LIKE, EITHER DISTRIBUTING THEM IN CLUMPS ALONG THE A LINES, OR SPREADING THEM OUT MORE EVENLY. EACH OF THE CIRCLES IN THE DIAGRAM AT LEFT REPRESENTS AN OBJECT IN THE ARRANGEMENT PICUTRED ABOVE (SEE STEP 4).

1. PAINT AND DECORATE POT

Cut a headline from the clippings to decorate the wide rim of the pot. Cut several other clippings in various sizes, and spray them with Make It Acid-Free! Let dry. Drybrush some white paint loosely over the outside of the pot and let dry. Using the brush and glue, add the newspaper clippings. Apply the gold finger pot rub to the rim of the pot. Glue on bits of shredded pieces of twine, then spray the whole pot with sealer.

2. CREATE FALSE BOTTOM AND ADD SAND

Tape over the hole in the bottom of the pot with packing tape. Create a false bottom using the scrap newspaper or bubble wrap, and pour in the scented sand. (For tips on making scented sand, see the Scented Sand Bowl, page 120.)

3. CREATE BACKGROUND FOR POT

Cover two or so additional newspaper photos or articles with contact paper or laminating sheets and trim to size. Place votives in the holders and place two of them in the sand, reserving one for the outside. Place the contact-covered photos on the surface where you would like to display your piece. Set the large pot on top of the contact-covered photos. Place the third votive candle on one photo in front of the sand-filled pot.

4. PLACE ITEMS FOR DISPLAY

Set additional postcards or photos in the pot by sticking a corner or an edge into the sand. Scatter a few tumbled brick pieces around the base of the pot. Add a grouping of moss, rocks and shells to the sand in the pot. Notice the final "A" shape of the composition, when viewed straight-on rather than from above.

nature

Bringing natural elements into the home creates a soothing reminder of our connection to nature. Découpage artists can utilize the many gifts nature has lavishly offered for the taking to create a natural sanctuary that incorporates outside elements into indoor living. In this section, there are projects that are inspired by natural scenes—a bird in flight in the Bird Canvas (page 40), and a beautiful depiction of deep blue hydrangeas on the Hydrangea Terra Cotta Pot (page 36). There are also projects that use nature's products to create art—the Maple Leaf Wood Round (page 50) uses a stamped leaf adhered to a log round as its central image, and the Nested Column (page 44) recreates a quaint nest with natural materials.

All of the projects in this section will also teach you useful new techniques for making the elements you incorporate into your designs appear naturally weathered. You'll learn how to distress wallpaper and stickers and how to tatter standard floral acetate ribbon, infusing all of the elements you use with character and personality. You'll also learn how to add another layer of interest with metallic finger pot rubs to highlight natural beauty.

hydrangea
terra cotta pot

grow \grō\ *v* to spring up and develop to maturity

Flowers have always been popular in home décor design—especially roses and hydrangeas—for adorning everything from linens to upholstered furniture and china. During times when a particular flower is popular, you will see many home accessories available with that design. For example, pansies enjoyed vast popularity a few years ago, and poppies, sweet peas and nasturtiums are now in vogue. When incorporating floral designs into your découpage projects, look for paper with an interesting background, as well as a clear focal point. This napkin's background has a printed and aged crackle effect that adds another dimension of interest without adding another technique to the project.

MATERIALS AND TOOLS

- standard 8" (25cm) terra cotta pot
- hydrangea-print napkins (Keller-Charles)
- standard white #3 satin acetate ribbon, 1 yard (90cm)
- stamp with text (or image)
- black inkpad
- white flat paint (Apple Barrel Plaid)
- Crafters Metallic Charcoal spray paint (Krylon)
- Home Décor Satin Blue Wisp spray paint (Krylon)
- metallic finger pot rubs
- water-based glue, thinned
- Matte Preserve It! spray (Krylon)
- foam brush
- rubber gloves
- disposable bowl (for paint)

from one artist
to another

CRAFTERS OFTEN VIEW THE TERRA COTTA POT AS A BLANK CANVAS BECAUSE IT HAS SO MUCH DESIGN POTENTIAL. THE HYDRANGEA POT WITH TEXT IS JUST ONE VERSION OF TERRA COTTA POT ART. IF YOU CHOOSE A NAPKIN WITHOUT A CRACKLE-EFFECT BACKGROUND, YOU MIGHT CONSIDER ADDING A CRACKLE FINISH. THIS PROJECT CAN ALSO BE DONE ON AN UNPAINTED POT FOR A COMPLETELY DIFFERENT BUT EQUALLY LOVELY LOOK. WHILE WHITE PAINT GIVES THIS PROJECT A CONTEMPORARY AND FRESH FEEL, TERRA COTTA IS BEAUTIFUL IN ITS OWN RIGHT AND WOULD CONTRIBUTE INTEREST TO THE DESIGN WITH ITS IMPERFECT SURFACE.

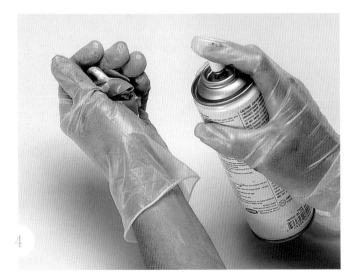

1. **PAINT TERRA COTTA POT WHITE**
Paint the terra cotta pot white inside and out with the foam brush.

2. **TEAR OUT HYDRANGEA IMAGES**
Tear out three sets of hydrangea images, making each one about 6¼" (17cm) tall by 5½" (14cm) wide. Angle the tears to create an irregular pattern, leaving one flat edge to butt up to the lip of the pot. Tear out images large enough to cover roughly two-thirds of the pot. Peel off the back ply of each image.

3. **ADHERE HYDRANGEAS TO POT**
Determine where you would like to place the first hydrangea image and use a foam brush to apply a layer of the thinned glue (two parts glue to one part water) to that area. Remove all excess glue from the brush before applying it. Adhere the image to the pot, adding more glue as needed. Make sure that the image ends before the bottom rim of the pot. Dip the brush into the glue-and-water mixture and run it lightly over the adhered image. Blot off any extra glue and smooth out any wrinkles. Rotate the pot a one third turn and repeat for the remaining images.

4. **ANTIQUE RIBBON**
Wearing gloves, crumple the white ribbon in your hand and spray it with the Home Décor Satin Blue Wisp spray paint. Move the ribbon around to distribute the paint, then crumple it and spray it with the Metallic Charcoal paint. Straighten it out to see if the paint has created a random, aged effect. Repeat if necessary.

5. **STAMP RIBBON**
After the paint dries, stamp the ribbon with your text stamp. Vary the orientation of the stamp, and use both light and heavy coatings of ink. Stamp randomly on both sides of the ribbon until the desired look is achieved.

6. **HIGHLIGHT WITH BLUE METALLIC FINGER POT RUB**
Pick up some blue metallic finger pot rub on your index finger and rub it around the rim and in the places where the hydrangea images meet the pot. Highlight a few raised areas with the metallic finger pot rubs as well.

7. **SPRAY POT WITH PRESERVATIVE**
Spray pot with Preserve It! to secure the metallic finger pot rubs.

8. **TIE ON RIBBON**
Tie the ribbon around the top lip of the pot and secure it with a bow. You can also tie the ends in a simple knot and let them dangle down for a different look. Fray the ends of the ribbon with your fingers.

bird canvas

soar \sor\ *v.* to sail or hover in the air, often at a great height; to rise to majestic stature

While a handmade look is wonderful, we want to hold ourselves to a high standard when crafting home décor accessories in order to maintain an excellent level of design. To achieve the same look as items available for sale, a handcrafted piece must have a good design and should be in line with the current trends. This simple and beautiful project allows even beginner crafters to create a piece of art that looks like it came straight from a home décor shop. I have a particular fondness for the palette of greens, browns, creams and whites in the bird image used in this project and for the artist's serious rendering of the bird. Feel free to choose another image in this same palette—for instance, an image of a stag in a forest—and pair it with an acorn stamp.

from one artist to another

TEMPERATURE WILL MAKE A DIFFER-ENCE IN THE EFFECT CREATED BY THE WAX. THE HOTTER THE WAX, THE SMOOTHER THE APPLICATION. USING THE BRISTLE BRUSH ADDS TEXTURE, AND YOU CAN ALSO BUILD UP LAYERS FOR A DIFFERENT LOOK.

MATERIALS AND TOOLS

- 8" × 10" (20cm × 25cm) ready-made primed canvas (Fredrix)
- bird images from scrapbook paper (Plaid)
- nest stamp
- black inkpad (Plaid)
- large manila tag
- 1 oz. unbleached beeswax
- ½ cup joint compound
- dark brown oil stain (Early American Minwax)
- découpage medium (Mod Podge by Plaid)
- electric gluepot
- 2 bristle brushes
- foam brush
- soft cloth
- butter knife (for spreading compound)

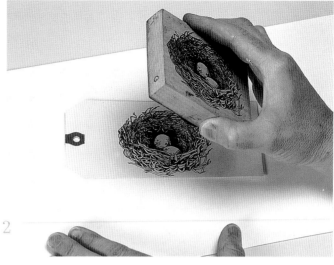

1. **TEAR OUT IMAGES AND STAIN CANVAS**
Cut or tear out bird images from scrapbook paper, leaving wide margins. Use the foam brush to apply stain to the canvas by angling the brush along the outside edge of the canvas.

2. **STAMP TAG**
Stamp the tag with the nest stamp. Ink the stamp evenly and test on scrap paper by pressing with steady pressure and being careful not to rock. Apply the stamp, centered lengthwise onto the tag. (Remember, if you smudge simply turn your manila tag over and start again.)

3. **APPLY JOINT COMPOUND AROUND IMAGES**
Using découpage medium and the bristle brush, apply the stamped tag to the canvas, centering it on the lower half of the canvas. Adhere the bird images over the rest of the canvas, overlapping the tag in places. Using a knife, spread joint compound in the spaces between the images, covering some edges of the images. Run the knife edge over the compound one final time to level it off. Allow joint compound to dry.

4. **APPLY WAX OVER JOINT COMPOUND**
Melt the beeswax at about 190°F to 195°F (200°F is too hot). Use a new bristle brush to apply the wax in a crisscross fashion over the canvas, covering the bird image with a very thin layer of wax. (Don't leave much of the image uncovered by wax, as the paper will absorb the stain and obliterate image details.)

5. **APPLY STAIN OVER WAXED AREAS**
Force some stain into the wax crevices with the foam brush. Make sure to leave some open, unstained patches in various spots over the entire canvas.

6. **REMOVE EXCESS OIL AND BUFF WAX**
Remove the excess oil with a soft cloth, buffing the wax gently.

Bird Plaque

Birds, nests, eggs and acorns are strong décor themes. This bird image is similar to one I've used when designing items for my home décor line. It works well on cones, too (see the Wall Cone, page 82). To continue the theme found in the bird image, you can create a "nest" inside the cone using some of the materials found in the Nested Column project (page 44). Fill your nest with candy eggs or, as a gift, fill it with chocolates or "little things I love about you" notes.

nested
column

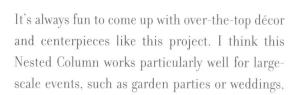

nest \ *n* a shelter prepared by an animal and especially a bird for its eggs and young: a place of rest, retreat, or lodging

It's always fun to come up with over-the-top décor and centerpieces like this project. I think this Nested Column works particularly well for large-scale events, such as garden parties or weddings, where decorations need to be oversized in order to have impact. To adapt this piece to decorate for a wedding, simply place a pair of Nested Columns in staggered heights at the ends of pews, on focal tables or at room entrance points. Have fun in your planning, and don't let conventional rules hold you back from exploring new methods and ideas. Like an actual bird's nest, this re-creation is contrived of loosely gathered, free-flowing materials, which give it an authentic look. This poignant piece is especially suitable for decorating events that symbolize new beginnings, such as weddings, baptisms and baby showers.

MATERIALS AND TOOLS

- 6" × 24" (15cm × 61cm) stovepipe
- 6" (15cm) round cap, to fit tapered shaft of stovepipe
- butterfly wallpaper (Tracy Porter)
- butterfly stickers ("Flight of Fancy," Tracy Porter)
- "Decorative Capital" stickers (Tracy Porter)
- 1¼ yards (90cm) no. 9 acetate ribbon, hunter green
- a generous yard (90cm) silver grid garland
- silver Mylar thread
- robin's eggs (found at craft stores)
- acorn letters to spell "N-E-S-T" (see Resources, page 126)

- Silver Shiver Webbing spray (Krylon)
- anchor tape (floral)
- floral wire
- spray adhesive (Super 77 by 3M)
- hot glue gun and glue sticks
- double-sided tape (optional)
- Fun-Tak
- sandpaper
- scrap newspaper
- vinegar and rag (to wipe oily residue from stovepipe)
- nippers
- ruler
- craft knife

- sturdy scissors
- pliers
- permanent marker (any color)
- pencil

NESTING MATERIALS:

- fun fur
- reindeer moss
- root vine
- waxed string
- sparkly fiber (Silver Cloud)
- excelsior
- long branches

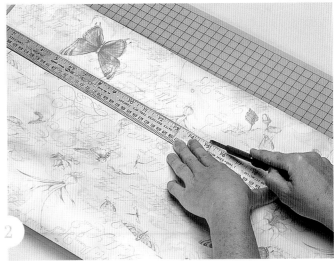

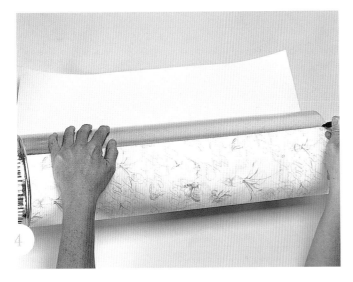

1. **DEPRESS DIMPLE**
Turn the cap upside down and use pliers to press the dimple tip on the bottom of the cap back in to prevent the piece from rocking when upright.

2. **CUT WALLPAPER TO FIT PIPE**
Place the butterfly wallpaper on a cutting surface, and cut it with a craft knife to a size that fits around the pipe (22" × 24" [56cm × 61cm] minimum), with about 2" (5cm) of overlap for tucking into the pipe at the top. Be sure the pattern is facing the right direction.

3. **WRAP WALLPAPER AROUND PIPE**
Using vinegar and a rag, wipe oily residue from the stovepipe. Wrap the wallpaper around the stovepipe, and make sure that the images are correctly aligned. Leave the grooved end uncovered.

4. **ADHERE WALLPAPER TO PIPE**
Release one end of the wallpaper and mark the pipe with a permanent marker. Spray one edge of the wallpaper with Super 77 and tack it to the stovepipe using the mark that you made before as a guide. Wrap the wallpaper around the pipe and adhere it with Super 77 or double-sided tape. As you position the wallpaper, remember that the seam on the stovepipe will show through in the finished project. You can choose to incorporate the seam into your design, or you can place it at the back.

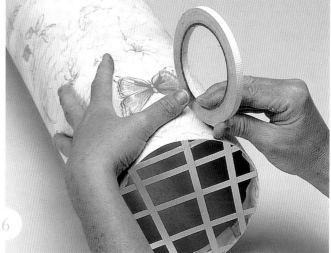

5. **SECURE WALLPAPER AT TOP OF PIPE**
Wrap the extra paper at the top of the
stovepipe over the top edge. The residual
stickiness of the wallpaper should be sufficient to secure the paper.

6. **MAKE GRID**
Insert the covered stovepipe into the cap.
Make a grid with anchor tape in the top opening of the stovepipe, spacing the strips of tape
about 1¼" (4cm) apart.

7. **ADHERE AND SAND WALLPAPER AND
LETTER STICKERS**
Spell out "HOME" with the letter stickers,
keeping the word straight by measuring up
from the bottom or down from the top and
penciling in a few guide marks. Place butterfly
stickers all around the papered stovepipe,
incorporating them into the wallpaper design.
Take a piece of sandpaper and rub over the
stickers so that some of the wallpaper shows
through—there should be breaks in the color
and design of the stickers, and the sanding
will dull the sheen of the stickers as well. Also,
sand the wallpaper so that it looks worn and
dull in places. You may sand the ridge created
by the seam in the pipe for extra distressing.

8. **SPRAY WITH WEBBING SPRAY**
Spray the tube sparingly with the Silver Shiver
Webbing spray. It's very easy to go overboard
with this spray, so you will want to practice on
scrap paper first. Hold the can at a distance of
12" (30cm) and spray (for demonstration purposes, I am showing the can closer).

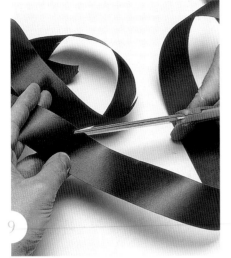

9. **CUT RIBBON**
Cut 1½ yards (1.35m) of hunter green ribbon. Using scissors, cut slits into the middle of the ribbon in a few spots. Randomly cut slits into the edges of the ribbon as well, varying the angles of the cuts.

10. **TATTER RIBBON**
Using the cuts as starting spots, rip and tear pieces of thread from the ribbon. Save the shreds for later use.

11. **TIE RIBBONS AROUND PIPE**
Tie the aged hunter green ribbon, the silver garland and the fun fur around the bottom of the stovepipe. Tie a piece of silver garland around the top of the stovepipe and cut off any extra material.

12. **BEGIN TO BUILD NEST**
Take a section of root vine and hot glue it around the very top of the stovepipe, on top of the silver garland.

13. CREATE NEST

Take a long section of root vine and make a tight coil, working from the inside to the outside to make the body of the nest. Rest the nest at an angle on top of the tape webbing so that the back of the nest is a little higher than the front edge. Begin weaving and tucking bits of silver garland, fun fur, sparkling fiber, leaves, shreds from the green ribbon and the other nesting materials into the root vine nest. Rest the nest on top of the grid you made with the floral tape.

14. FINISH NEST

Tuck some curved branches into the weave of the root vine in a pleasing composition so that some of the branches are sticking up and out of the nest. After placing the branches, secure them with a few drops of hot glue.

15. PLACE EGGS AND HANG ACORNS

Cut four 3" (8cm) lengths of floral wire and bend them at both ends to create an "s" shape. Twist one end of each wire around some of the root vine, tucking it up and under the nest. (You may hot glue the wire to the nest to keep it from slipping.) Space the hooks about ½" (1cm) to 1" (3cm) apart. String each lettered acorn on varying lengths of waxed string, and tie the two ends in a knot at the top. Hang each acorn on a wire hook to create a staggered effect that spells out "N-E-S-T". Twist the hooks to position the letters, and tie the final piece of waxed string holding the "T" in a bow. Place the robin's eggs in the nest. Use a bit of Fun-Tak to keep the acorns in a readable position (flat against the pipe), if desired.

THE HERBALIST

4

tterish taste. The balsamic juice
ollected in Canada in shells, and
to Europe under the name of Ta
haca. Alcohol, or spirits, is the proper
solvent. The Populus Balsamifera is
generally confounded with the Populus
Candicans, from whose buds we get the
virtues known as the Balm of Gilead,
but it is much the superior tree for
medical purposes.

Properties and Uses—The buds have
been employed internally as a stimulant
orant but now seem to be used
al purposes as counter-
ments and

L NASTURTIUM Cress.
—Water Cress, and roots.
Leaves ourtium grows
anching stems
erally ex-
The

maple leaf
wood round

earthen \ˈər-thən\ *adj* **made of earth, earthly**

For me, and I think for most Oregonians, it is impossible to live without being devoted to, and learning a great deal from, nature. The pioneers who first ventured into the West were pursuing a dream of a better life with imagination and creativity, and it was on this principle that the modern West was formed. To this day, many people living in the West retain a strong, soulful connection to the land. Relationships with nature provoke an organic approach to design requiring one to continually seek new ideas. Nature's spontaneous influences keep things fresh, exciting and relevant, providing us with a tinderbox of inspiration and education. The Maple Leaf Wood Round symbolizes this closeness to nature—it is designed to reflect both the wildness and the beauty found there.

MATERIALS AND TOOLS

- 7" (28cm) wood round with bark intact (Walnut Hollow)
- sawtooth hanger
- leaf images from nature, color copied
- gold cording or copper wire, 2½ yards (2.25m)
- feathers or other embellishments
- classic alphabet stamps (All Night Media)
- black inkpad
- Apple Butter Brown antiquing medium (Plaid)
- sandpaper
- small foam brush
- découpage medium, matte finish
- Preserve It! (Krylon)
- piece of computer paper (for paint)
- disposable plate or paint palette
- hot glue gun and glue sticks (optional)
- scissors
- paper towel

from one artist to another

RATHER THAN USING ALPHABET STAMPS TO ADD YOUR WORD TO THE LEAF, YOU MAY USE YOUR COMPUTER. COPY YOUR LEAF AND PRINT THE WORD OVER THE IMAGE. TO INSURE PROPER PRINTING PLACEMENT ONTO YOUR LEAF, SIMPLY PRINT THE ENLARGED WORD ON A SAMPLE PIECE OF PAPER. NEXT, STACK THE TWO PAPERS, ONE ATOP THE OTHER WITH ALL OF THE EDGES ALIGNED. HOLD THE PAPERS UP TO A BRIGHT LIGHT AND SEE WHERE THE WORDS WOULD PRINT ON THE LEAF. MAKE ANY NECESSARY ADJUSTMENTS.

1. **STAMP AND CUT OUT LEAF IMAGE**
   Make a color copy of a leaf you've found. Using black ink, stamp the copy with the word "JOY" or with another word or phrase of your choosing. Spray the stamped image with Preserve It! and allow it to dry. Cut out the stamped image with scissors.

2. **POUNCE PAINT ON WOOD ROUND**
   Determine which side is the best side of the wood round and turn it so that the good side is facing up. Crinkle up the piece of computer paper to create some stiff peaks. Dip it into the antiquing medium and blot off the excess paint onto the paper towel. Pounce the paint in a continuous movement onto the wood round so that the flecks are evenly spaced.

3. **SAND PAINTED SURFACE**
   After the paint dries (wait several minutes), lightly sand the surface of the wood round to move the paint tone into some of the open, porous spaces.

4. **ADHERE LEAF IMAGE**
   Use a foam brush to apply a thin layer of découpage medium to the back of the leaf image and center the leaf on the wood round. Smooth the cutout down to adhere it to the wood round. Add a little découpage medium to any irregular edges that are not sticking to the wood. Make sure to wipe away any excess medium on top of the leaf. Try to keep margins the same at the widest points of the leaf. There will not be a "perfect" center, so just move it around until it looks good to you.

5. **TWIST FEATHERS INTO CORDING**
Cut a length of gold cording or wire to about 2½ yards (2.25m), and twist the feathers or other embellishments of your choice into it at regular intervals. (Or you may hot glue the embellishments to the cording.) Position the feathered cord horizontally above the stamped word and hold it in place with one hand.

6. **FINISH WRAPPING GOLD CORDING**
Wrap the cord and feathers around the wood round both vertically and horizontally in a random pattern. The gold cording should intersect at several points, but the stamped word should always be clearly visible.

7. **SECURE GOLD CORDING AND ADD SAWTOOTH HANGER**
Twist the ends of the gold cording together in the back to secure the wrap. (As you wrap the gold cording or wire around the wood round, be careful not to pull it too tightly.) Add a small sawtooth hanger to the back of the finished wood round.

Twine-Wrapped Wood Round

For a different, all-natural look, you can wrap your wood round with simple brown twine. In keeping with the 100% natural theme, you could even découpage the actual pressed leaf onto the wood round, rather than making a copy of it.

The office or dignity of a
magistrate; the body of magistrates. — **magistrate**, n.
A public civil officer, in-
vested with the executive or
judicial authority. — **magis-
tratic**, maj-is-trat'ik, a.
magnanimity, mag-na-nim'-
i-ti, n. Greatness of soul or
mind; not selfish.—
magnanimously, adv.
magnate, mag'nāt, n. A
great man; a person of rank
or wealth.
magnesia, mag-nē'si-a, n. A
soft white slightly alkaline
powder.— **magnesium**

retro

While different people have different things in mind when they say that
something is "retro" in style, the term most simply means that the piece is
making use of a bygone trend associated with a certain era. Several different
time periods are considered retro when used in design today. For example,
1950s, 60s and 70s retro includes the looks commonly called "Mid-Century
Modern," and also the "Space Age" and "Atomic" styles that were popular
from the 40s through the 60s, inspired by orbital shapes and other images
and materials created through the space program. Retro kitsch—a term used
to describe items which were first thought of as hip and stylish, then later
considered tacky or in bad taste, and which are now generally found quirky
and charming (although there are detractors in both camps at any given
time)—is another look commonly associated with the 1950s, 60s and 70s.

Another design category that is often considered retro is the vintage
style, which originated in the 1920s, 30s and 40s. By definition, vintage
means an original from this era, but the term is often used to describe a
worn element of a design, or to describe an item that looks like it came from
a "vintage" era. As in any style, the boundaries are blurred between one style
and another. Some of the projects in this section combine different retro
elements. Chocolate and pink polka dots give the Garden of My Youth project (page 68) a 70s retro feel, and the aging techniques coupled with the old
window frame contribute a tattered vintage element. Two of the other projects, the S'mores House Call Toolbox Kit (page 60) and the Retro Runner
(page 56), evoke more of a 50s, kitschy feel. And the Reliquary Box (page 64)
has a purely vintage feel.

retro runner

Maybe it's because we have long been such a mobile society that we seek a better balance between a life of routine and a life of excitement. We remember the days of our youth brightened by the building anticipation of vacation—an earned reward for our labors—and as adults we continue to crave that excitement. So, to conjure up those great memories of childhood vacations, you could incorporate lots of old items like Texaco road maps and old color ephemera from the 50s in addition to vacation photos. As découpage elements, personal mementos really spur on the imagination and pay tribute to family legacies. This project also works well for commemorating other events, such as a graduation celebration. Use pictures and memorabilia from recent childhood and teenage years to make your own keepsake runner, coasters or placemats.

MATERIALS AND TOOLS

- prime canvas cloth, cotton primed (12" × 48" [30cm × 122cm])
- copied black-and-white photos (add black photo corners before copying)
- silver charms (retro travel theme, see Resources, page 126)
- 2 old slides
- white rickrack
- black yarn
- various retro rubber stamps (PSX—Road Trip)
- black inkpad (Stamp-A-Memory Archival Dye Inkpad)
- black acrylic paint, thinned to a watery consistency (a bit thicker than water)
- black permanent marker with wide tip
- eyedropper
- deckle-edge scissors
- pinking shears
- scissors
- ⅛" (3mm) hole punch
- foam brush
- découpage medium (Aleene's Instant Découpage Glue Matte Sealer is recommended for best results)
- Preserve It! (Krylon)
- yardstick (or ruler)
- eyelet-setting tool
- ⅛" (3mm) black eyelets
- hammer
- paper towels
- pencil
- paper plate or palette
- iron

from one artist to another

FAVORITE PHRASES AND NICKNAMES CAN BE APPLIED TO THE RUNNER IN PLACE OF RUBBER STAMPS. PRINT PHRASES ONTO REGULAR COMPUTER PAPER AND CUT AWAY EXCESS, LEAVING A NICE MARGIN. BLACKEN THE EDGES WITH A WIDE PERMANENT MARKER AND CUT ALONG THE EDGES WITH DECKLE-EDGE SCISSORS OR PINKING SHEARS. LET THE INK DRY THOROUGHLY AND TREAT THE BITS OF TEXT WITH PRESERVE IT! JUST AS YOU DID WITH THE PHOTOS. ALLOW PRESERVE IT! TO DRY THOROUGHLY BEFORE APPLYING DÉCOUPAGE MEDIUM TO THE PHOTOS.

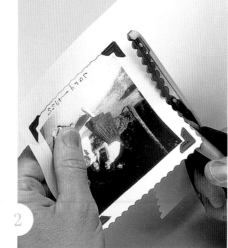

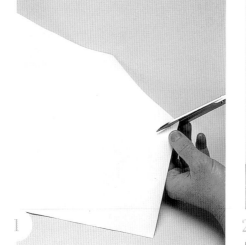

1. **CUT CANVAS CLOTH**
Cut the canvas cloth to 12" × 48" (30cm × 122cm), and cut each end into a point.

2. **COPY AND CUT PHOTOS**
Place black photo corners on each photo and make black-and-white photocopies. Cut them out with deckle-edge scissors. Spray the pictures with Preserve It! and allow them to dry.

3. **PLACE AND ADHERE PHOTOS**
Make sure the runner is bright side up and position your pictures on it. Stamp various images in the spaces between the pictures. (Refer to the finished photo for placement ideas.) Then découpage the photocopied photos onto the runner using a foam brush and the découpage medium. Apply the medium to both the backs of the photos and to the canvas.

4. **SPATTER RUNNER WITH BLACK INK**
Add water to a little black paint and mix them together. Fill the eyedropper with the mixture and test it on a scrap piece of paper. The paint should be blackish gray when it dries. Add more water until the desired color is achieved. To spatter the ink, tap the dropper gently against your finger. Spatter ink all over the runner, letting some fall on top of the pictures and on top of the stamps. Allow paint to dry.

5. **OUTLINE RUNNER EDGES IN BLACK**
Place the ruler parallel to the runner's edge, about ¼" (6mm) from the edge. Using the black permanent marker with the wide tip, make a black border around the entire runner using the ruler as a guide.

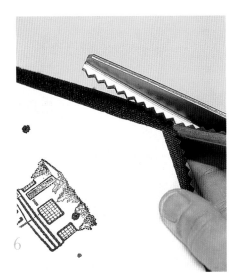
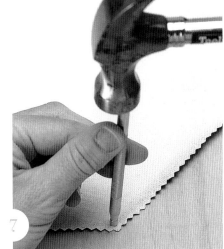

6

7

8

6. CREATE DECORATIVE BORDER

Use the pinking shears to create a patterned
edge on the black border.

7. SET EYELETS

At each pointed end of the table runner, attach
three eyelets, one at each point of the "trian-
gle" (for a total of six holes). Hit a hole-
punching tool with a hammer to make a hole,
positioning the hole so that it is surrounded by
a black border. Insert an eyelet from the front
to the back. Turn the piece over and hit the
eyelet-setting tool with a hammer until the
eyelet shaft spreads and the eyelet is set.

8. TIE ON ACCENT PIECES

Set eyelets in each slide. Cut six 15" (38cm)
lengths each of white rickrack and black yarn.
Age the rickrack with the black paint mixture
and let dry. Tie the slides and charms onto the
runner with the yarn. Tie the rickrack in a bow
around the yarn. When the runner dries, iron
the backside to smooth out any buckling.

handy tip

WHEN PLACING PICTURES, MAKE IT EASIER ON
YOURSELF BY NUMBERING EACH PICTURE LIGHTLY
ON THE BACK AND PENCILING IN A CORRESPONDING
NUMBER ON THE CANVAS. ADHERE THE PICTURES ONE AT
A TIME TO THEIR NUMBERED SPOTS. PLACE PHOTOS AT
VARYING ANGLES ON THE CANVAS, AVOIDING CREATING
PARALLEL LINES. YOU SHOULD BE ABLE TO VIEW SOME
PHOTOS "CORRECTLY" FROM ANY VANTAGE POINT.

Retro Placemats and Coasters

*Placemats and coasters require additional découpage
medium for gentle cleaning purposes. (Again, it's important that you have used Preserve It! on your photos and
have allowed them to dry thoroughly.) Brush découpage
medium slowly in a very thin layer over the entire surface
of the photo, letting each layer of glue dry thoroughly
before applying the next. Apply two or three coats.*

s'mores house call
toolbox kit

I've recently rediscovered s'mores—those delightfully crunchy, gooey, chocolatey campfire sandwiches. Unfortunately, I've also discovered that they can be made in the microwave, and now I want them far too frequently. And, though I've yet to know the joy, I know for a fact that some people have even added caramel. S'mores conjure up cozy images of campfires and crisp fall nights, and you can bring that feel to an ordinary toolbox by adding scrapbook papers with a vintage theme that are easily found at the local scrapbook or craft store. One paper that works well is Retro Campfire Girl, which is widely available on scrapbook paper. Simply fill the decorated toolbox with all of the neccesary supplies and you're ready for any s'mores emergency.

MATERIALS AND TOOLS

- toolbox, 19½" × 6" × 3½" (50cm × 15cm × 9cm) (Master Mechanic)
- retro images (ripped from Two Busy Moms scrapbook paper)
- letter tiles (from an old board game or from a scrapbook store)
- oil stain (Early American by Minwax)
- découpage medium, matte finish
- interior/exterior Leather Brown gloss spray paint (Krylon)
- Fun-Tak (for positioning images)
- 2 small foam brushes (one for oil stain, one for glue)
- super glue gel
- all-purpose remover, like Goof Off or Oops (optional—for removing labels and wiping off excess spray paint)
- rubber gloves
- craft knife with very sharp, new blade

from one artist
to another

IN MUCH THE SAME WAY THAT BEAUTIFUL CHINA AND HANDSOME FILE FOLDERS CAN INFUSE THE MUNDANE TASKS OF WASHING DISHES AND PAYING BILLS WITH JOY, THIS TOOLBOX WITH ITS ARTFUL SPIN CAN LIGHTEN OUR APPROACH WHEN CONTEMPLATING THOSE LITTLE FIX-IT JOBS THAT COME UP FROM TIME TO TIME. VERY ORDINARY OBJECTS ARE REJUVENATED WITH THE SIMPLE USE OF PAPER, PASTE AND PAINT.

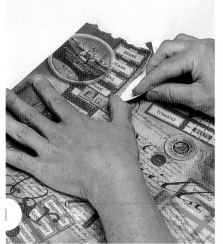

handy tip

IF YOUR FOAM BRUSH IS TOO WIDE TO FIT INTO THE CAN OF OIL STAIN, JUST CUT THE SIDES OF THE BRUSH SO THAT IT FITS EASILY INTO THE CAN.

1. **TEAR OUT IMAGES**
   Rip images out of the scrapbook paper. Choose about ten to twelve images in various sizes.

2. **STAIN EDGES OF RIPPED IMAGES**
   Dip your foam brush into the stain, making sure to get all of the excess stain off. Tap the brush gently around the edges of the image to stain it. Repeat with all of the torn-out images.

3. **POSITION IMAGES ON BOX**
   Arrange the stained images in a pleasing composition, tacking them onto the toolbox with Fun-Tak. You may overlap images to add interest. It's okay to position pieces over the box opening—you can use your craft knife to cut them apart later. Leave a spot in the top center of the box to place your letter tiles arranged to spell the word or phrase that you've chosen.

4. **ADHERE IMAGES TO BOX**
   Adhere each image to the box individually (leave all of the pieces attached to the box with Fun-Tak except for the one you are applying). Remove any single image and use a foam brush to coat the back of it with a thin layer of découpage medium, and adhere it to the toolbox. Repeat for all of the images. As you glue on the images, wipe off any excess glue so that it does not turn the surface of the toolbox a cloudy white.

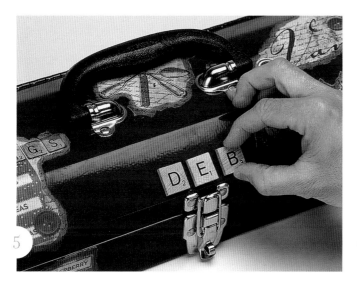

5. **ADHERE LETTER TILES TO BOX TOP**
Place the letter tiles you chose in the center of the toolbox lid with Fun-Tak to make sure they are spaced properly before adhering them. Place a small dot of super glue gel in the back center of each piece and adhere the pieces to the box in the desired position. You may need to hold the pieces in place for a few moments if the super glue is not bonding instantly.

6. **SPATTER TOOLBOX**
Before spraying the toolbox, practice directing and spattering the paint on a scrap piece of cardboard. Using very slight pressure, depress the trigger on the spray paint can slightly to splatter the toolbox with the brown spray paint. To slow the paint flow, you can hold the can upside down. You may use Oops or Goof Off to remove unwanted splatters from the metal box, but it will not remove paint from the images, so be careful not to spray the images too heavily.

7. **CUT THROUGH IMAGES BLOCKING BOX OPENING**
When the images are partly dry, run the blade of the craft knife in the groove between the lid and the tray of the toolbox so that the images do not hold the box closed. Make sure the razor goes all the way through the paper—but be careful, the sharp blade may tear the damp images if pulled through too quickly.

handy tip

To save yourself some work, place paint-brushes in plastic bags and tie them off with a twist wire between uses. Keeping the brushes sealed up will keep the paint or stain from drying out and will also enable you to continue to use your brush without washing it. This handy trick also works well with the larger rollers used to paint large areas.

reliquary box

reliquary \re-lə-kwer·ē\ *n*
a container where relics are
stored or displayed (especially
relics of saints)

Celebrating our lives through décor provides us with an opportunity to create a home that both feeds the spirit and comforts the body. With shrines and altars we make a connection through materials to our own souls and inner sources of strength. I find it humbling and enlarging for my own spirit to acknowledge the relics of our lives and those of loved ones. Simple historical objects become revelations of a life's destiny, taking on different meanings when viewed in retrospect. Filling a handcrafted reliquary box with sentimental talismans can lift us beyond what, oftentimes, feels like an ordinary existence, nudging us to recall our purpose of grace and hope. Gather your most precious mementos—or relics, if you will—and place them inside your box when you finish. Remember to open it up on occasion and renew yourself by revisiting past moments.

MATERIALS AND TOOLS

- slider-top box, any size (Walnut Hollow)
- brushed nickle handle with appropriate-length screws (home improvement centers)
- vintage-style scrapbook paper with script
- plain white paper to print definition (see page 67)
- old cloth tape measure (may bleach new one to achieve an aged look)
- alphabet stencil in typeset style
- all-purpose white interior/exterior spray primer (Krylon)
- Greek Stone gloss spray paint (Krylon Interior/Exterior)
- black acrylic paint
- strong coffee in a misting bottle
- bristle brush
- foam brush
- ¾" (2cm) stencil brush
- metallic finger pot rubs (optional)
- sandpaper
- slightly thinned water-based glue
- drill and drill bit to fit handle
- pencil

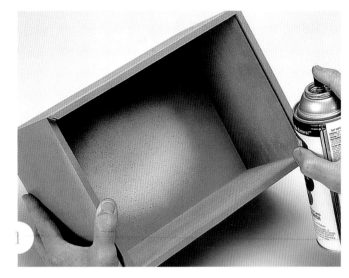

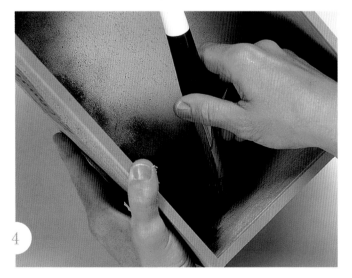

1. **PAINT SLIDER-TOP BOX**
Spray paint the box and lid with the all-purpose white primer and allow to dry. Spray paint the slider-top box and lid with the Greek Stone spray paint. As you spray paint, create a faded look by applying the paint in a somewhat light layer. On the inside of the box, avoid spraying the primer in the bottom center of the box, leaving an open white oval. Be sure to paint inside the slider groove.

2. **TEAR OUT IMAGES AND SAND BOX**
Tear out enough images in varying sizes and shapes to cover most of the box. Make sure to tear out one larger image to place on the lid of the box. Sand over the entire box to take off some of the shine and to smooth out any bumps in the wood.

3. **ADHERE IMAGES TO BOX**
Using the foam brush and the découpage medium, adhere the images randomly to all sides of the box and to the lid. Create a balanced composition by wrapping some images around corners and by varying the placement of images in the upper and lower portions of the sides of the box.

4. **PAINT INSIDE EDGES OF BOX**
Dip the stencil brush into some water and then into the black paint to thin it. Wipe off the excess paint. Pounce the brush along the inside edges of the box, blending the area between the greenish gray paint and the white primer.

5. **SAND EDGES OF BOX**
Sand the edges of the box and the edges of the images, especially at the corners where the images meet. Also, sand the box in random places to show some wear. You may also sand the inside of the box to dull any black paint that appears too heavy.

6. **ADD DEFINITIONS AND STENCIL**
Make 2-3 copies of the definition of the word reliquary (at right), and stain it with coffee by soaking it, letting it dry, and then misting it with coffee again. (Depending on the darkness of the desired effect, soak the paper for up to three or four minutes and mist it immediately afterwards.) Let the paper dry. Tear out the stained definitions, leaving ragged edges. Découpage the stained and torn pieces onto the box in random places on the outside of the box and on the lid. Using the alphabet stencils and the stencil brush, paint in the word "RELIQUARY" on the top of the box with black paint.

7. **ADD FINISHING TOUCHES TO BOX**
Position the handle in the front center side of the box and mark the spots for the holes with a pencil (usually 3" [8cm] from center of screw hole to center of screw hole). Drill two holes in the marked spots, and attach the handle. You may need to replace the screws that come with your handle with shorter ones. Take the cloth tape measure and tie it in a bow around the reliquary box as a finishing touch.

handy tip

MAKE A COPY OF THIS DEFINITION AND STAIN IT WITH COFFEE FOR YOUR RELIQUARY BOX.

Reliquary: a container where relics are stored or displayed (especially relics of saints)

garden *of my youth*

sentimental sen-ta-men-tal *adj* influenced by tender feelings

Recently, when we took a family trip to a ghost town called Golden, my grown son Austin picked a simple sweet pea bouquet and presented it to me without fanfare. It was one of those rare, fleeting times when Austin the man briefly became a little boy again. It was a beautiful gesture on a beautiful day—you might say it was sweet, or you could even say golden. This specimen box is meant to preserve the unexpected treasures of our lives. In fact, one of the sweet peas from my son's impromptu bouquet was pressed and used here. As you create your own specimen box of memories, feel free to use anything that resonates with you. For other specimen boxes, I've used pages quickly and crudely torn from magazines, acorns, special tokens, glitter, spun tinsel and found objects. I've scrawled verses on manila tags and attached them as well. Make your specimen box unique to you, a pleasant reminder of the simple joys in your life.

MATERIALS AND TOOLS

- old window frame (salvage yards, antique stores, recycle centers)
- foam core cut to fit window opening
- retro-style scrapbook paper (pink-and-brown polka dot)
- floral image (Dover clipart)
- word stickers (Rebecca Sower)
- butterfly rub-on transfers (Tulip)
- "Alphabet Stickers" (Tracy Porter)
- classic alphabet stamps (All Night Media)
- various colored metal-rimmed tags
- white vellum metal-rimmed tags
- white mini bags, size 4" × 2½" (10cm × 6cm)
- waxed string
- cotton balls
- dried or pressed flowers
- pressed petal stickers
- old postcards and other ephemera (make copies to preserve originals)
- "furry" pink fun string (found with fishing supplies)
- fine iridescent glitter

- gold Mylar thread
- silk daisy heads
- decorating chalks
- quilting pins
- crimson inkpad
- oil pastels
- water-based glue
- clear gel tacky glue (Aleene's)
- spray adhesive (Super 77 spray by 3M)
- Preserve It! (Krylon)
- photo-mount squares (clear), or glue gun or glue dots
- bristle brush (for chalks)
- foam brush
- sandpaper
- hot glue gun and glue sticks
- hole punch
- craft knife
- measuring tape
- pencil
- cutting mat
- scissors

from one artist to another

I CHOSE TO DISPLAY THIS COLLECTION OF MEMENTOS INSIDE A WINDOW FRAME BECAUSE OF THE RICH SYMBOL-ISM IMPLIED IN "WINDOWS." VINTAGE WINDOW FRAMES ARE FUN, TEMPORAL FLIGHTS OF FANCY, PROVIDING A METAPHORICAL BRIDGE BETWEEN THE PAST AND THE PRESENT. A VINTAGE WINDOW FRAME WITH ITS OLD HARD-WARE PLACED ON THE WALL IN MY HOME CONTINUALLY MOTIVATES ME BEYOND ANY DESIGN LIMITATION, INSPIRING ME TO PUSH MYSELF BEYOND MY BOUNDARIES.

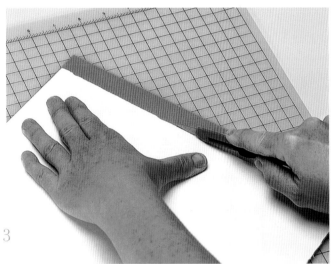

handy tip

WHEN USING SPRAY MOUNT TO ADHERE THE PAPER TO THE FOAM CORE, SPRAY THE BACK OF THE PAPER INSTEAD OF SPRAYING THE FOAM CORE SO THAT YOU'LL HAVE MORE CONTROL WHEN YOU ADHERE THE PAPER TO THE FOAM BASE.

1. **MEASURE FRAME**
Measure the window frame vertically and horizontally to determine the size of the foam "window pane."

2. **CUT FOAM CORE AND ADHERE PAPER**
Cut the foam core to fit the window frame's measurements. Adhere one piece of polka dot paper to the foam core with Super 77 spray. Determine the position for the second piece of polka dot scrapbook paper by placing it on the foam core so that the pattern of the alternating polka dots continues as seamlessly as possible from one piece of paper to the next. Make a light line with a pencil to mark the correct position for the second piece of paper.

3. **ADHERE SECOND PIECE OF PAPER AND TRIM EXCESS**
Adhere the second piece of polka dot paper using spray adhesive, aligning it with the line you've drawn. Erase any visible pencil line, if necessary. Turn the covered foam core over and place it on a cutting mat. Trim away the excess paper by carefully running the blade of a craft knife along the edge of the foam core.

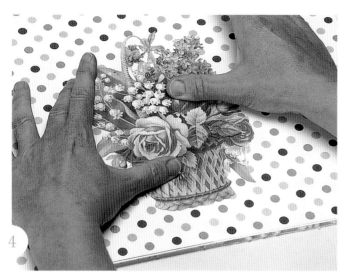

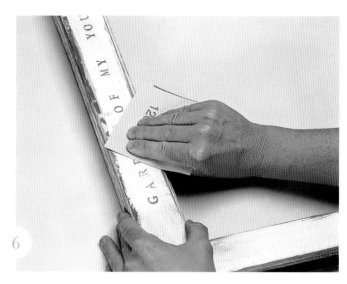

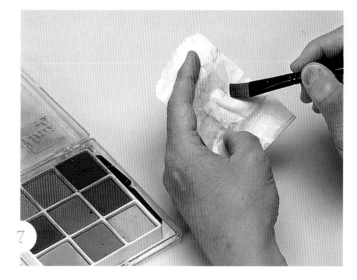

4. ADHERE FLORAL IMAGE

Enlarge the flower basket from the Dover clipart book 125% or to the desired size, and cut it out with scissors and a craft knife. Turn the cut-out image over and spray it with Super 77. Adhere it to the polka dot–covered foam core, centering it over the paper seam.

5. STAMP PHRASE ON FRAME

Before stamping, lay out the letter stamps to spell "GARDEN OF MY YOUTH" across the top of the window frame to ensure proper spacing. Stamp the phrase across the top of the frame using the crimson inkpad. While you are using the inkpad, stamp the word "SPECIMEN" on a vellum tag.

6. SPRAY AND SAND STAMPED PHRASE

Spray the stamped phrase with Preserve It! Sand the stamped and sprayed phrase with sandpaper until parts of the letters are missing and the wood shows through in places. Turn the window frame over and fit the paper-covered foam core snugly into it. Run a line of hot glue around the edges of the foam core to secure it to the window frame.

7. BEGIN DECORATING BAGS AND TAGS

Adhere letter stickers to make various words on some of the tags (see photo of finished project for ideas). Add other stickers to the tags as well, if desired. Crinkle up two mini white bags in your hand. Use the small flat paintbrush and the palette of chalks to go over the bags, coloring the creases. Stuff a cotton ball into each bag, and then tie a tag around the neck of the bag with waxed string.

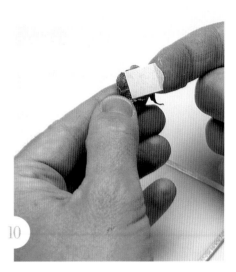

8. **CHALK DAISIES**
   Using the same technique as in step seven, apply a light dusting of chalk to the petals of the daisies.

9. **CHALK PINK "FURRY" STRING**
   To tone down the bright color of the pink furry string, lay it directly in the palette of chalks and rub the paintbrush in the chalks and over the yarn.

10. **ADHERE PHOTO-MOUNT SQUARE TO DRIED PETAL**
    Hold a dried and pressed petal in your fingers face down, and adhere a photo-mount square to its back. (You may also use a glue gun or glue dots here.)

11. **ADHERE DRIED PETALS TO TAGS**
    Turn the petal right-side-up and adhere it to a tag, pressing down gently to secure. Punch a hole in one side of the tag and tie on the pink furry string.

terms of endearment

ANY PHRASE, LINE FROM A POEM OR TERM OF ENDEARMENT COULD BE STAMPED ALONG THE TOP EDGE OF AN OLD WINDOW FRAME. CHOOSE A PHRASE THAT IS A LOVING REMINDER OF SOMEONE OR OF SOME SPECIAL EVENT. STAMPING THE DATE OF YOUR SPECIAL EVENT CAN ALSO ADD EXTRA INTEREST AND CONNECTION.

12. POSITION DECORATIVE ELEMENTS

Begin to position all of your elements on the polka dot paper, spacing them around the central floral image. Move all of the pieces around in different spots until a pleasing and balanced composition is found.

13. SECURE DECORATIVE ELEMENTS

Using the quilting pins, secure each decorative element to the papered foam core so that it is suspended about ¼" to ½" (6mm to 1cm) away from the background, creating a three-dimensional effect. Add a few butterfly rub-ons to the frame corners and pin an additional daisy to the frame, if desired. Glue bags on with dots of glue.

14. ADD COLOR WITH OIL PASTELS

Choose a complementary shade of oil pastel and run it along the inside of the frame to add a bit of color.

15. SPRINKLE ON GLITTER

Using a paintbrush or foam brush, paint a small amount of clear gel tacky glue onto the frame. Sprinkle a little iridescent glitter over the glue as a finishing touch. Weave bits of gold Mylar thread lightly around the pins to add a little sparkle.

romantic cottage

Romantic home décor is characterized by a comfortable yet polished and refined style in a predominately muted or soft color palette. The Romantic style incorporates a wide range of colors in many different tones—including pink in all of its incarnations, of course. In all of its shades, pink expresses romance beautifully. A pink embrace recently began with mauve in the 80s when combining mauve, burgundy and hunter green to create a Victorian look was popular for home décor. This burgundy and mauve movement morphed into the softened rose hues with worn fabrics and furnishings that became the style now known as Shabby Chic. From there pink has grown white hot! The ubiquitous use of pink reflects energy, sass and femininity. In this section, delicate pastel pinks appear in the endearing Romantic Letter Box (page 86) and in the sentimental design of the Altered Life Journal (page 76). If you want to spice up your projects, you can incorporate more surprising tones like hot pink or watermelon into the design.

Along with the muted color palette, the Romantic style usually incorporates a profusion of candles and sparkling embellishments. Candelabras and single candlesticks bring an opulence that is so much a part of the Romantic look. And, by adding crystals to decorative elements like chandeliers, candelabras and pillows, lush contrast is created to the matte finishes found in the cozy fabrics and on the painted, distressed furniture used in many relaxed styles. For instance, the easy Wall Cone (page 82) features crystals and iridescent elements that add lift and dimension.

altered life
journal

Altered books make wonderful canvases for self-expression and are often intimate and personal works, crafted primarily to nurture the creator. This altered journal, however, is designed for a broader expression of your personal life and incorporates family and friends into its pages. It is meant to declare milestones by using each new chapter page to symbolize another phase in the interlacing lives of different family members. For example, Chapter 1 might have childhood images of the family matriarch and patriarch. Chapter 2 might find pictures of both the bride and the groom as young single adults; and Chapter 3 might express the celebration of their wedding, with many more chapters to come. In charting the course of our lives, we become aware of the blessings we have been given. Combine the tradition of preserving the past in scrapbooks with the freedom of designing altered books to create a history of your family's blessings and life passages.

MATERIALS AND TOOLS

- book with interesting "romantic" cover or shabby chic fabric to cover book
- shabby roses scrapbook paper
- netting from fruit bags
- florist's wire (18" [46cm])
- standard white wedding corsage flowers
- 2 yards (1.8m) pink velvet ribbons
- vintage-style floppy narrow pink and blue pastel ribbon (Romance Ribbons, see Resources, page 126)
- vintage velvet leaves
- pink, white and iridescent rhinestones
- white paint (Apple Barrel by Plaid)

- pink spray paint (you can use the soft pink Crackle Ballerina paint from the Romantic Letter Box project)
- pink metallic finger pot rubs or pink paint
- water-based glue
- wax paper
- rubber gloves (optional)
- Make It Last! (Krylon), if using Crackle Step 1 spray paint
- Preserve It! (Krylon)
- bristle brush
- hot glue gun and glue sticks
- scissors

FOR INSIDE PAGES:

- vintage-style tag with floral image (Scrappy Chic)
- various embellishments (photo anchors, brads, tags)
- various old pictures (theme-based)
- ephemera (old matchbooks, postcards, etc. in a pink palette)
- crinkle ribbon (to tear and distress)

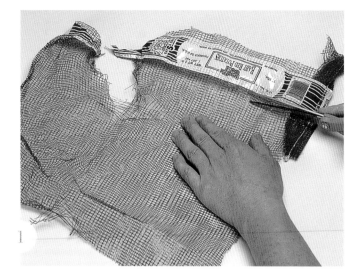

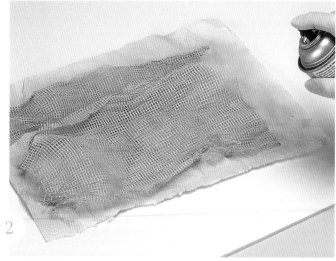

1. **CUT FRUIT BAG NETTING**
Using scissors, cut out the front of the fruit bag to about 3" × 18" (8cm × 46cm). Once painted, the netting is reminiscent of the kind of nettings often used in vintage hats—it will serve as the foundation for the bow.

2. **SPRAY PAINT STRIP OF NETTING**
Paint the strip of netting with pink spray paint. Depending on the color of the fruit bag, you may consider allowing some of the original color to show through. Spray the painted netting with Make It Last! to keep the pink paint from flaking.

3. **CREATE BOW FOUNDATION**
Scrunch the top of the painted netting together and create a loop with the top third of the piece, allowing one tail to stick up behind the loop. Allow the remaining two thirds of the netting hanging down for a second loop and tail. Twist the florist's wire through the loop and around to the back to secure it.

handy tip

NEW ROSE-PRINT FABRICS MAY BE AGED TO SUBDUE THEIR ORIGINAL BRIGHT INTENSITY BY SPRITZING THEM WITH A DILUTED BLEACH MIXTURE, GIVING THEM A WASHED AND WORN APPEARANCE. THIS CAN BE USED TO GREAT EFFECT ON VELVET AND VINTAGE VELVETEEN RIBBONS TOO. YOU WILL WANT TO EXPERIMENT ON SMALL PIECES FIRST; THERE IS SOME UNPREDICTABILITY IN THIS PROCESS.

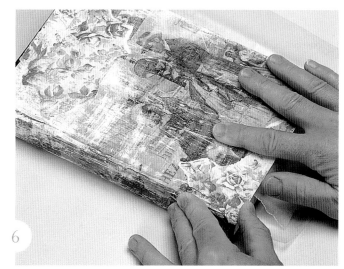

4. **DRYBRUSH BOOK COVER**
Drybrush white paint over the cover with a bristle brush, making sure the brush is almost completely dry. Leave some of the title showing, and brush the paint on in vertical and horizontal strokes. Make sure to paint the inside flaps of the cover.

5. **ADHERE SHABBY ROSES PAPER**
Tear out about three pieces of complementary scrapbook paper (two for the front, one for the back) and brush glue onto the back of each piece. Make sure to leave a straight edge on each piece and align them with the top and bottom edges of the front cover and with the top or bottom edge on the back cover.

6. **GLUE COVER ONTO BOOK**
Glue the cover onto the book using glue. Begin by applying glue to the inside back flap of the paper cover and also to the back flap of the book cover. Continue gluing in this manner, moving from back to spine to front cover to front flap until the cover is completely adhered to the book. Slide a piece of wax paper between the wet back and front flaps and the pages of the book to prevent sticking.

7. **CUT VELVET RIBBON AND TACK ONTO BOOK COVER**
Cut a one-yard (90cm) length of the pink velvet ribbon to be tied around the book just below the midpoint (it will be used to tie the book closed). Tack the ribbon to the book cover on the front and back of the book using small dots of hot glue.

8

9

10

handy tip

If you're having trouble picking up the rhinestones, just lick your finger before you pick one up. The rhinestone will stick to your finger.

8. **BUILD NOSEGAY**

Make several loops using the pink velvet ribbon (three or four loops on each side of the bow, as in a florist's bow). Secure the bow with wire. Glue the loose velvet bow on top of the pink netting bow with a dot of hot glue. Insert the vintage velvet leaves between the loops of the velvet bow. Make a multi-looped floppy bow with the vintage-style pink pastel ribbon, and glue it to the nosegay with hot glue.

9. **ADD CORSAGE FLOWERS AND RHINESTONES TO NOSEGAY**

Lightly spray the white corsage flowers with the pink spray paint. If you're using the Ballerina Make It Crackle! paint, follow with a topcoat of Make It Last! to prevent flaking. Tuck the flowers into the nosegay to add finishing touches. To create sparkle and depth, adhere rhinestones to various spots on the nosegay using small dots of hot glue.

10. **ADD PINK METALLIC FINGER POT RUB HIGHLIGHTS (OPTIONAL)**

Wearing rubber gloves, dip your finger into the pink metallic finger pot rub or pink paint. Run the rub onto the edges of the book that show through at the edges to soften the color. Spray Preserve It! over the metallic rubs to seal them.

11. **ATTACH NOSEGAY TO BOOK COVER**
Apply a generous amount of hot glue to the center back of the nosegay, and adhere it to the top left of the book cover. You should still be able to see a little of the title. Trim netting if necessary.

When attaching brads and all other things that need to pierce your page, pierce through more than one page (2-4 pages is sufficient) for a secure, tight hold without any fear of eventual ripping.

what does it all mean?

TODAY, EVERYBODY USES THE TERM "EPHEMERA." SO WHAT DOES IT MEAN, EXACTLY?

THE FORMAL DEFINITION SAYS THAT THE TERM EPHEMERA REFERS TO THE TYPE OF OBJECTS WHICH, WHEN THEY WERE PRODUCED, WERE NOT INTENDED TO LAST A LONG TIME OR WERE SPECIALLY PRODUCED FOR ONE OCCASION. WHILE THIS COULD MEAN ALMOST ANYTHING, IN THE CRAFTING WORLD WE'RE ALMOST ALWAYS REFERRING TO PAPER ITEMS—LIKE TICKET STUBS, PROGRAMS, CARDS, INVITATIONS, ETC. YOU CAN COLLECT YOUR OWN PERSONAL EPHEMERA, FIND IT IN FLEA MARKETS AND ANTIQUE SHOPS, OR YOU CAN BUY IT IN SCRAPBOOKING AND CRAFT STORES.

It is a fun idea to use every chapter to tell a story, but it is not necessary. Your book will become very thick if you intend to do several artwork pages. You must remove excess pages (be sure to keep "chapter" pages intact). Use a craft knife with a ruler placed behind the last page to be cut, at the spine, in order to avoid cutting through the wanted pages. (Do all cutting before starting to adhere your artwork.)

With Valentine Greetings

wall cone

Roses and other floral motifs are dominant themes for the Romantic look, as well as the use of luxurious tactile elements. I've emphasized the opulent aspect of the style by giving this Wall Cone a light dusting of glitter and filling it with iridescent grass. Since the Romantic style is one part comfort and another part glitz, partnering the muted colors of the roses in the napkin with the shimmer of glitter and the decadence of the white feathery trim creates an interesting juxtaposition of color and texture. Hang this little cone on a doorknob filled with iridescent grass or use it as a decoration for a special occasion.

MATERIALS AND TOOLS

- 10" × 10" (25cm × 25cm) pre-primed canvas cloth (Fredrix)
- rose napkin, cocktail size (IHR)
- Peach Perfection acrylic paint (FolkArt)
- Light Pink acrylic paint (Apple Barrel)
- Pastel Pink acrylic paint (Apple Barrel)
- 1½ yards (1.35m) white feathery trim
- 3 iridescent buttons
- ⅔ yard (59cm) rose-colored crinkle ribbon (Romance Ribbons, see Resources, page 126)
- iridescent grass

- sparkle découpage medium (Mod Podge Sparkle)
- pouncing brush
- découpage medium (Mod Podge Glue Matte Sealer)
- hot glue gun and glue sticks
- foam brush
- paper towels
- scissors
- pencil
- ruler
- disposable plate or paint palette

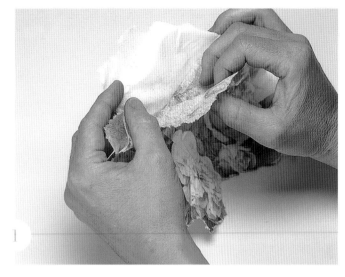

sugar and spice and everything pink

U SING A FEW SPARKLING ELEMENTS IS A GREAT WAY TO CREATE A
MAGICAL ATMOSPHERE FOR A YOUNG GIRL'S SPECIAL OCCASION.
FROM CHANDELIERS, SUSPEND CLEAR OR PINK CRYSTALS OR BEADS,
PINK BALLET SLIPPERS FILLED WITH IRIDESCENT SHRED, BLACK-
AND-WHITE COPIES OF PICTURES FROM RECITALS OR SCHOOL, DIS-
TRESSED RIBBONS AND WIRED STEMMED ROSES. PLACE BALLET
TUTUS OVER DINING CHAIRS, STREW IRIDESCENT SHRED, PINK OR
IRIDESCENT GLITTER AND ROSEHEADS ON OTHER SURFACES IN THE
ROOM. FILL A CRYSTAL OR GLASS BOWL WITH SHRED OR GLITTER,
AND ADD PICTURES OF YOUR YOUNG LADY FROM HER INFANCY AND
CHILDHOOD, INCLUDING FRIENDS AND FAMILY.

1. **CUT CONE, TEAR OUT ROSE IMAGE**
    If your canvas is not yet cut to size, trim it to
    10" × 10" (25cm × 25cm). Then place the 10"
    (25cm) mark of your ruler diagonally at one
    corner of the canvas, marking several spots at
    the 10" (25cm) radius to create an arc line.
    Connect the marks to make an arc. Trim along
    the arc line to make the cone shape.

    Open the rose napkin and tear out around the
    rose cluster, leaving a little of the cream back-
    ground. (I've left out the blue part of the
    image.) Make sure the image is large enough
    to cover a significant amount of the canvas,
    leaving a little of the canvas showing. The
    biggest part of the image should cover the
    front center of the canvas. Tear off the back
    two plies of the torn-out napkin image.

2. **DÉCOUPAGE IMAGE ONTO CONE**
    Apply the plain découpage medium to the can-
    vas with a foam brush and adhere the roses,
    smoothing the image by working from one
    side to the other or from the center to the out-
    side. Dab glue on top of the image to take care
    of any wrinkles. Don't worry if you rip the
    image—little imperfections add a worn ele-
    ment. Let dry.

3. **APPLY MOD PODGE SPARKLE AND
    CREATE CONE**
    Trim off any overhanging edges. Using a foam
    brush, randomly apply some Mod Podge
    Sparkle to different areas of the roses. Glue
    the seams together with hot glue to form a
    cone. Overlap the seams so that the image
    edges come together in a pleasing way.

4. ADD PAINTED HIGHLIGHTS

Stuff paper towels into the cone to help it hold its shape while you add painted highlights. Pour three quarter-sized puddles of each paint onto a palette or disposable plate. Pounce the brush into all three colors and work the mixture into random areas. Apply some paint in areas where there is no image. Add additional highlights with Peach Perfection.

5. WRAP TRIM AROUND CONE

Cut a piece of the white feathery trim and tack it at the back seam with a dot of hot glue so that some of the ribbon is above the cut edge of the cone, hiding the cut edge. Continue gluing the feathery trim around the rim of the cone with the hot glue gun. Cut off extra trim.

6. ATTACH CRINKLE RIBBON HANDLE

Make a twist in the rose-colored crinkle ribbon about 2" (5cm) from the end. Glue the ribbon to the sides by pressing the twist of the ribbon into a dot of hot glue on each side.

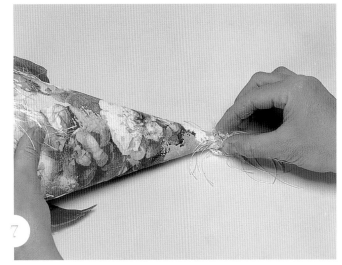

7. WRAP TRIM AROUND BOTTOM

Cut a piece of feathery trim (about 1¾" [4cm]) to fit around the bottom of the cone, and hot glue it into place.

8. ADD FINISHING TOUCHES

Glue on the iridescent buttons, placing one over each side where the ribbon is adhered (over the twist) and one over the feathery trim. Glue iridescent grass at each button and fill the cone with the grass, letting some stream down the sides.

romantic letter box

cherish \cher-ish\ *v.t* to entertain or harbor in the mind deeply and resolutely

For this sentimental box I used an ornate image found in the pages of an old dictionary. I've always been intrigued by dictionaries, and spent hours flipping through them as a young girl. I love dictionaries and old textbooks not only for their wonderful educational value—they also provide endless artwork for vintage papercrafting. The combined old elegance of the image and the soft pink crackle paint in this project seem to speak of sweet innocence and young love. The final touch for the box—the delicate pink ribbon—is aged with coffee. As you begin staining, you may as well make a pot from a nice grind. When you're done you can sit back and enjoy a cup while admiring your new old letter box. Things can sometimes work on all levels, don't you agree? In addition to the ribbon, you may also age the paper with coffee for this project, though I have not. I recommend a light coffee or tea stain to set off these delicate paint colors.

MATERIALS AND TOOLS

- cigar box (large enough to accommodate image)
- bird-and-flourish image, page 88
- baby-pink acetate ribbon, no. 2 size (4 yards [3.6m])
- strong coffee in spray bottle with mist setting
- Make It Crackle! Step 1, Vanilla Icing (Krylon)
- Make It Crackle! Step 2, Ballerina (Krylon)

- Apple Pink acrylic paint (Apple Barrel)
- Peach Perfection acrylic paint (FolkArt)
- water-based glue, thinned slightly
- Make It Last! (Krylon)
- ¾" (2cm) stencil brush
- foam brush
- sandpaper
- paper plate or palette

from one artist **to another**

The thicker the coat of Make It Crackle! Step 2 that you apply, the more dramatic the crackle effect will be. Just make sure not to let the paint dry while you are spraying it. If you apply multiple layers of Step 2, the crackle effect will not take place and you'll have to start over with Step 1.

Bird-and-Flourish

Enlarge this pattern until desired size is reached.

1. **SAND BOX AND SPRAY WITH STEP 1**
Make sure that all of the labels are smoothly attached to the surface of the cigar box so that there are no rough edges sticking up. Sand down any unruly edges. Remove any nails. Spray the cigar box with Step 1, Vanilla Icing, both inside and out. Spray the box with two to three coats to get a solid covering. After the Step 1 dries, look over the box again to make sure that no stickers or tags are sticking out. If you find any aberrations, sand those places lightly. Spray the box again with Step 1. Let each coat dry before applying the next.

2. **SPRAY WITH STEP 2**
When the final coat of Step 1 has dried (allow about half an hour), spray the box with Step 2 of the crackle process, Ballerina. Spraying the bottom and the inside first, apply a light to medium coat of Step 2 (thick enough to coat well, thin enough that it doesn't run). It is helpful to jack up your box by setting it on a small brick, leaving the edges free of contact with other surfaces.

3. **COPY AND TEAR OUT BIRD-AND-FLOURISH IMAGE**
Spray the box with Make it Last! Copy the bird-and-flourish image on this page, following the copying instructions. Tear out the image in one piece, leaving jagged edges and margins around it.

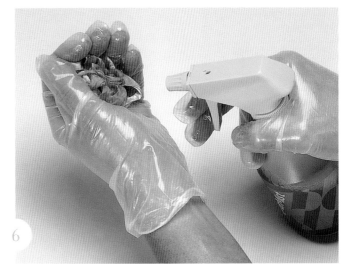

4. **ADHERE PAPER ELEMENTS TO BOX**
Thinly coat the backs of the images using the foam brush and the thinned glue (three parts glue to one part water). Découpage the bird-and-flourish image onto the top of the box, centering it from its widest points. Make sure all of the edges are tacked down securely. If desired, find a favorite quote or phrase and découpage the text onto the front bottom of the box, centering it below the lid where the box opens (as pictured).

5. **CREATE PINK HIGHLIGHTS**
Dip the stencil brush into the Apple Pink paint and pounce it around the image and the phrase, blending the paint. Pounce the brush lightly over a few random spots of the image. Use the same brush to pick up some Peach Perfection paint, blending the colors. Pounce the brush lightly over about seven to eight places to create some warm highlights.

6. **ANTIQUE RIBBON**
Place the ribbon in water to saturate it. Wring out the ribbon and crumple it in your hand. Fill a misting bottle with strong coffee and spray the crumpled ribbon. Continue to turn the ribbon in your hand as you spray, leaving some pink showing. Lay the ribbon flat, mist it with more coffee and let it dry.

7. **WRAP RIBBON AROUND BOX AND TIE**
Wrap the ribbon around the box several times, allowing it to cross in several random places. Tie the ends in a knot and fray and rip the ends to make the ribbon look worn.

old world french

Old World French style infuses new inspiration into traditional uses of aged surfaces by combining them with heavy weaves, tassles and rich textures to create a romantic atmosphere. Aged architectural elements, such as crumbling stucco and fresco walls and the worn stone of majestic buildings, have inspired mottled painted and glazed surfaces seen on everything from dishes and linens to furniture. This aged effect is the concept behind the Pour Toi Tin (page 96) layered with wax, stain and plaster. The French Wine Clock (page 102) also has an aged effect created by simple torn edges and blended paints.

The French themes and neutral palette of the projects in this section make them a perfect fit with many of the other styles presented in this book. The elegant element of sparkle, as found in the Eiffel Tower Wall Hanging (page 102) would coordinate with the recently defined Parisian Apartment style, which might be most easily understood as a combination of Shabby Chic and European décor.

french wine clock

Grapes and wine have long been associated with European style and are very strong themes in current home décor trends. Butter-colored paints are also very popular right now, and when coupled with the grape images in this project, they create a warm softness and a clean, fresh feel. By blending and mottling the paint, you'll learn how to incorporate the images "into" the clock face. As finishing touches, I've added black clock hands that remind me of wrought iron and have more heft (appearance of weight) to them than brass hands. You may also add black numbers at every quarter to coordinate with the clock hands and to create a heavier, less delicate feel.

MATERIALS AND TOOLS

- 11½" (29cm) wooden disc with hole (Walnut Hollow)
- clock hands, black (Walnut Hollow)
- clock movement, Quartz TQ700P (Walnut Hollow)
- grape images from napkins (Caspari) (or other French images)
- Camel acrylic paint (FolkArt)
- Taffy acrylic paint (FolkArt)
- Antique Gold Metallic paint (FolkArt)
- Burnt Sienna acrylic paint (Apple Barrel Plaid)
- découpage medium
- sandpaper
- bristle brush
- ¾" (2cm) stencil brush
- no. 12 flat paintbrush
- level (optional)

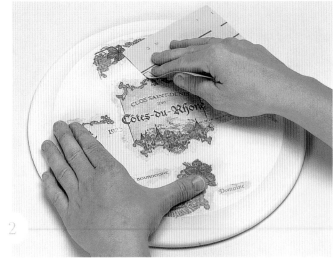

handy tip

REMEMBER TO TAKE YOUR IMAGES WITH YOU TO THE CRAFT PAINT SECTION TO HELP WITH MATCHING THE IMAGE BACKGROUND TO THE PAINT COLOR. MATCHING THE COLORS CLOSELY WILL HELP THE IMAGES BLEND INTO THE BASE BACKGROUND.

1. **DÉCOUPAGE IMAGES ONTO CLOCK**
Paint both sides of the wooden disc using the bristle brush and Taffy paint. Let dry. Tear out images for the center and four quadrants of the clock face. Peel off the back layers of the napkin images so that only one ply remains. Using the bristle brush and the découpage medium, begin applying the images, starting with the large one in the center. Place the other images at noon, three, six and nine o'clock. Make the lettering on the images as straight as possible, using a level if you like.

2. **SAND EDGES OF DISC AND IMAGES**
Lightly sand over the images and the edges of the wooden disc. If the images have wrinkles, sand those down as well.

3. **POUNCE ON HIGHLIGHTS**
Begin pouncing Taffy paint onto the disc in random areas, making sure to add some color along the edges of the images. Next, with the Camel paint and the stencil brush, randomly pounce color in a few areas of the background, blending in some with the images. Repeat the process with just a bit more of the Taffy to lighten up some of the darker areas.

4. **PAINT RIM OF CLOCK**
Brush the rim with Burnt Sienna, carrying the color over the rim to the back of the clock. If you get any paint onto the center area of the clock, it can be sanded off a bit when it's dry.

5. **ADD GOLD HIGHLIGHTS**
Randomly drybrush gold metallic paint over the Burnt Sienna in a few places.

6. **ADD CLOCK MOVEMENT AND CLOCK HANDS**
Sand over the inner rim of the clock to clean up any Burnt Sienna. Use a pencil to poke out the paper that is covering the hole in the center of the clock. Insert the clock movement into the hole from the back to the front. Attach the clock hands according to the instructions on the package.

handy tip

IF YOU CAN'T FIND A WOODEN DISC IN THE SIZE YOU WANT WITH A PRE-DRILLED HOLE, YOU CAN BUY A WOODEN PLATE AND MAKE YOUR OWN CLOCK FACE. SIMPLY TRACE THE DISC ON PAPER AND FOLD THE CIRCLE INTO QUARTERS, MATCHING UP THE LINES BY HOLDING THE PAPER UP TO THE LIGHT. THE CENTER IS WHERE THE CREASES MEET. LAY THE PAPER CIRCLE OVER THE DISC. MARK THE CENTER BY PUSHING A STRAIGHT PIN THROUGH THE PAPER AND INTO THE WOOD, AND THEN INSERT YOUR DRILL BIT.

OR, YOU CAN FIND THE CENTER OF THE DISC BY MEASURING THE DIAMETER OF THE CIRCLE AND DIVIDING IT IN HALF. MAKE A SMALL LINE WITH A PENCIL ABOUT AN INCH LONG AT THAT POINT. TURN THE DISC A QUARTER TURN AND REPEAT, DRAWING ANOTHER PENCIL LINE ABOUT AN INCH LONG. THE CENTER IS WHERE THE TWO LINES CROSS. USE A ⁵⁄₁₆" (2MM) DRILL BIT AND AN ELECTRIC DRILL TO MAKE A HOLE IN THE CENTER.

pour toi tin

This French-inspired tin is one of several designs that I created for Reed & Cross, a fine Oregon home décor shop. "Pour toi" translates to "for you," and stamped into wax and stained, it creates a romantic and nostalgic feel. The layers of plaster and stain added to the tin evoke the look of aged European walls. Toile images, which are depictions of finely detailed pastoral and allegorical scenes rendered on fabric, further create a French feel for this design. Surprisingly, the "toile" process originated not in France, but rather near Dublin, where country scenes were printed from copper plates onto a solid-color fabric background (usually black on white) using one color of ink. Now, toile is available on paper and in a selection of colors—usually red, blue or black on white or cream. Toile is an enduring classic that is widely used on home furnishings as well as on paper napkins and other decorative accessories.

MATERIALS AND TOOLS

- 5¾" × 11" (15cm × 28cm) galvanized tin pot (French floral tin)
- images from toile napkin (IHR) (scrapbook paper may also be used)
- French phrase stamp
- black inkpad
- alphabet metal embossing set
- Satin Touch Pebble spray paint (Krylon), or color to match napkin background
- Ivory Satin spray paint (Krylon)
- 1 oz. beeswax
- joint compound

- metallic finger pot rubs (aged brown)
- dark brown oil stain (Minwax Early American)
- Preserve It! (Krylon)
- découpage medium
- butter knife or spreading tool
- electric gluepot
- bristle brush
- small foam brush
- fine sandpaper
- vinegar and rag

from one artist to another

FOR THIS PROJECT I HAVE USED THE METAL EMBOSSING ALPHABET SET GIVEN TO ME BY MY DAD MANY YEARS AGO. HOWEVER, THERE ARE NOW SETS AVAILABLE AT MAJOR CRAFT STORES WITH A FEW REALLY WONDERFUL FONT STYLES TO CHOOSE FROM.

1. **CLEAN TIN AND PAINT OUTSIDE**
Clean the tin using the vinegar and rag. Paint the outside of the tin with the Ivory Satin spray paint. Make sure you coat the handles and the area around the handles well. No need to worry about running paint.

2. **SPRAY PAINT INSIDE OF TIN**
Paint the inside of the tin with the Satin Touch Pebble spray paint, giving it two to three light coats to achieve a nice, solid coverage and to avoid runs.

3. **ADHERE IMAGES TO TIN**
Rip images from the napkin or scrapbook paper, leaving the edges ragged. Tear out four images of separate vignettes, two different ones for the "front" and "back" sides of the tin. Peel off the back two plies of the napkin images so that the images are one-ply. Using the découpage medium and a foam brush, découpage the images onto the surface of the tin, placing the first image toward the top right of the tin and the second image to the left of the first, toward the bottom of the tin. Turn the tin to the other side and repeat this place-ment pattern for the remaining two images.

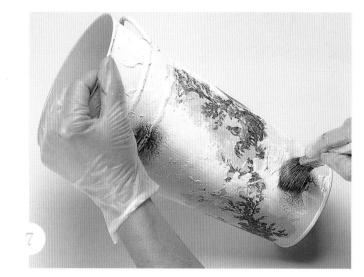

4. **APPLY JOINT COMPOUND TO TIN**
   Apply a thin layer of joint compound to the tin
   with a butter knife or similar spreading tool.
   Avoid layering the joint compound over the
   images, but you may drag the knife very lightly
   over them to add a little texture. Pick a spot to
   place your text between the two front images
   and between the two back images. Make sure
   to apply joint compound to those areas so that
   the ink from the stamp will bond properly.

5. **SAND TIN**
   Sand the tin, primarily where there is plaster.
   Be careful not to rub all the way down to the
   metal (there should not be any silver showing). Drag the sandpaper very lightly over the
   images so they are not distorted.

6. **APPLY WAX TO TIN**
   Apply a layer of wax over the images and in
   some of the open places between the joint
   compound (see Basic Techniques, page 10).
   Avoid waxing the plastered area where you will
   stamp the words.

7. **APPLY STAIN TO TIN**
   Dip a bristle brush or a wadded-up paper
   towel into the stain, and wipe away all of the
   excess stain. Leaving your chosen text areas
   open, apply some oil stain very lightly in a few
   random open spaces between images, working
   it in with a circular motion. Avoid staining
   the images.

8

9

10

handy tip

T RY A TEST RUN OF EMBOSSING LETTERS INTO LAYERED HOT WAX ON A PIECE OF CARDBOARD BEFORE YOU DO IT ON THE TIN TO GET A FEEL FOR THE RESISTANCE OF THE WAX AND ITS COOLING POINT. WHEN EMBOSSING THE LETTERS, YOU WANT THE WAX TO BE WARM, BUT NOT TOO HOT. A PRACTICE RUN WILL ALLOW YOU TO STRIKE THE RIGHT BALANCE.

8. **STAMP ON FRENCH TEXT IMAGE**
Press the French text stamp into the black inkpad and stamp the phrase onto the open spot between the two front images on the tin. Roll the stamp from right to left as you apply the image so that it adheres to the rounded surface. Repeat the stamp on the back side of the tin.

9. **BUILD UP THICK LAYER OF WAX**
Using the bristle brush, apply wax to the stained areas. Also apply the wax to other random areas on the tin and over the stamped words. Build the wax up in layers in the spot in the top center of the tin where you will emboss the letters. Apply at least seven or eight layers of wax as a base for your impressions. Before adding a new layer, wait until the previous layer has cooled a bit and clouded over. Let your last layer cool just a few moments before embossing it so that it is solid underneath, but still warm. To avoid runny wax, turn down the heat on the gluepot a little.

10. **STAMP TEXT INTO WAX**
While you are letting the wax cool just a bit (the wax will cling to the metal letters if it is too hot), arrange the metal embossing letters to spell the word or phrase that you will impress into the wax, in this case "PARIS". Place the letters within easy reach, and make sure they are facing the right way. Center the word between the top rim and the first ridge of the tin. Press each metal embossing letter firmly into the still-warm wax to leave the impression of the letter.

11. APPLY STAIN TO EMBOSSED LETTERS

Stir the stain vigorously. Work some stain into the impressions left by the embossing letters using either a fragment from a cut foam brush or a bristle brush. Force the stain down into the crevices and allow it to sit for a few seconds before wiping away the excess. Continuously work the stain into the letter impressions. Also stain the layered wax surrounding the letters. If the stain doesn't seem to be getting dark enough in the letter impressions, you can let the stain sit for up to an hour before wiping it away.

12. ADD METALLIC FINGER POT RUB

Wearing rubber gloves, dab your finger into the aged brown metallic finger pot. Smooth the rub along the top and bottom rims of the tin and along the handle tops. Spray the metallic rub with Preserve It!

bright idea

IF YOU ARE HAVING TROUBLE WITH YOUR UNDECORATED PILLAR CANDLES NOT BURNING IN THEIR ENTIRETY AND CHANNELING DOWN THROUGH THE CANDLE AS THEY SHOULD, YOU NEED TO CREATE "CANDLE MEMORY." WHEN LIGHTING YOUR CANDLE FOR THE FIRST TIME, LET IT BURN UNTIL THE ENTIRE TOP SURFACE HAS MELTED. EACH TIME THEREAFTER, LET IT BURN LONGER.

Pour Toi Candles

I was very excited when the idea for embossing the top of these candles came to me. It's a new twist on embossing in wax—instead of bringing the wax to the project, I brought the embossing to the wax. These candles are decorative and are not meant to be burned in their entirety. However, with care the center may be burned wide and deep enough to insert a votive candle.

eiffel tower wall hanging

recycle \rē-sī-kəl\ *v* to recondition and adapt to a new use or function; to use again, especially to reprocess

When I designed this rather metropolitan piece, I included elements from both French and Retro styles. In keeping with retro style, I used an aged surface—a piece of vintage molding—as my background, and added rustic details at the edges. To incorporate a contrasting surface texture into the project, I included crystal beads and old buttons. The resulting style of this piece is so sophisticated that admiring viewers will never guess how inexpensive it was to make. Salvage yards and recycle centers give you the most bang for your buck when shopping for interesting stuff to play with—vintage molding costs just pennies per foot. And better yet, the Eiffel Tower image comes from a purse-sized pack of ten facial tissues that yields 80 images, so you can make just one or several.

MATERIALS AND TOOLS

- salvaged molding (with original paint), 3¾" (10cm) tall and cut to a length of 4¼" (11cm)
- Eiffel Tower image from tissues or from scrapbook paper
- ⅔ yards (59cm) 18-gauge galvanized wire
- crystal beads or vintage buttons
- antiquing medium (Apple Butter Brown Plaid)
- water-based glue, thinned
- electric drill with 5/64" (8mm) drill bit (drill a hole big enough to accommodate wire)
- needle-nose pliers
- sandpaper
- small foam brushes
- ruler

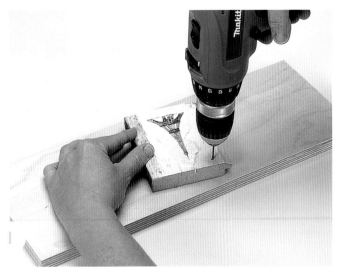

1. **TEAR OUT IMAGE AND DRILL HOLES**
    Clean the molding. Tear out your image to
    approximately 4" (10cm), making sure it fits
    on the molding. Leave a straight edge at the
    bottom of the image. Peel off all of the back
    plies. Drill one hole in each top corner about
    ¾" (2cm) in from each edge.

2. **ADHERE EIFFEL TOWER IMAGE**
    Découpage the Eiffel Tower image onto the
    center of the square of molding with the
    watered-down glue (two parts glue to one part
    water) and a foam brush. Brush a thin layer of
    glue onto the molding and place the bottom
    edge of the image directly along the bottom
    edge of the wooden piece. Smooth the image
    down. Then go over the image with the brush,
    saturating it.

3. **ANTIQUE MOLDING EDGES**
    Use a small foam brush to dab the antiquing
    medium along the edges of the molding. Make
    sure the freshly cut wood edges and corners
    get a good coating of antiquing medium.

4. **THREAD WIRE AND BEADS
    THROUGH FIRST HOLE**
    Cut a piece of wire to about ⅔ yards (59cm) and
    thread it through one hole in the molding
    from the back to the front. Pull about 1" (3cm)
    of wire through the hole. Slip a vintage button
    or a crystal bead onto the end of the wire and
    use the needle-nose pliers to begin to curl the
    remaining end of the wire to secure the bead
    or button to the front of the piece.

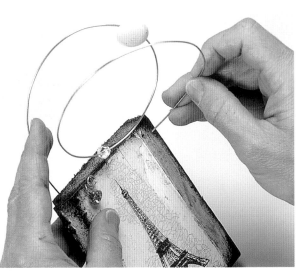

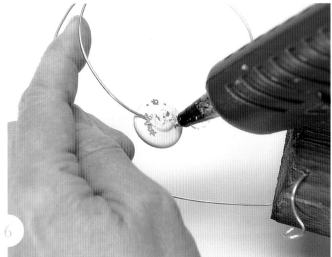

5.

6.

5. **THREAD WIRE AND BEADS THROUGH SECOND HOLE**

Finish shaping the end of the wire into a tight curl. Thread two to three buttons and/or beads onto the free end of the wire. Bring the wire up from the back and make two loose loops. Avoid kinking the wire. Bring the free end of the wire through the other hole from front to back, creating a hanger.

6. **SECURE BEADS ON WIRE**

Make another tight curl in the end of the wire with the pliers and bring it to the side so that the curl is visible from the front. Add dots of hot glue to the beads to secure them on the looped wire.

French Wall Hanging Grouping

The color palette of the pieces in your grouping may coordinate to tie them all together, or you may connect them by using different images on the separate pieces to tell a story. Collect travel ephemera such as maps, pictures and postcards of architecture, and cultural symbols (such as ticket stubs from museums and napkins from small cafés). You may even write descriptions on these pieces after your découpage medium has dried. Write your sentiment in brown pencil, or go over your final regular pencil line with a fine-tip black permanent marker. Erase any pencil marks.

zen

A whimsical interpretation of Asian style, the Zen look is easy to incorporate into typical Western homes. The Zen style is built on the concepts of balance, simplicity and meditation, which come directly from the principles of the Buddhist tradition. As Westerners, we have become increasingly aware of the importance of contemplation and reflection, and adding Zen touches to our décor offers a decidedly friendly and approachable way to be mindful of the needs of the soul and the body.

Homes decorated in the traditional Asian manner are often minimal in their furnishings, and focus on clean lines and rich, smooth surfaces. Traditional Asian style uses black and red as dominant colors to create crispness and punctuation. In Western interpretations, crispness and clean lines are still prioritized, but are often softened with natural greens, naturally hued weaves and natural materials, such as reeds and grasses. (Once again, nature becomes a common denominator.) The Scented Sand Bowl project (page 120) is a balanced, symmetrical design that pairs natural materials—wood and sand—with shiny galvanized tin. The Fortune Candle project (page 108) offers an amusing approach to the common ground found when East meets West.

IT'S NOT THE SIZE OF THE DOG IN THE FIGHT, IT'S THE SIZE OF THE FIGHT IN THE DOG

fortune candle

My husband and I are sentimental and find it hard to throw away little messages of good will, like the fortune cookie papers used in this project. We like to keep little reminders of every event, however insignificant. Besides saving fortunes from cookies, we keep concert and transfer tickets, and anything else of this nature. (We haven't kept the few speeding tickets we've gotten over the years for nostalgia's sake, however! *Au contraire!*) In designing for the home, the sentimental, humorous and often exceedingly generous nature of the crafter can provide the impetus for design.

MATERIALS AND TOOLS

- white glass pillar (sanctuary) candle (8¼" [21cm] tall)
- fortunes from fortune cookies (these may also be made on your computer)
- white mulberry paper with gold thread cut to 9" × 9½" (23cm × 24cm)
- thin gold cording, 4 strands each 40" (102cm) long, plus 2 feet (61cm) for tag
- Black Hills Gold Fiber (Silver Cloud)
- Oriental coins with square hole in the center (see Resources, page 126)
- text stamp with Chinese luck symbols (PSX)
- Chinese postage stamp stamp (Hero Arts)
- "To and From" stamp
- vellum tag
- gold inkpad (to match tone of gold cord)
- water-based glue
- small bristle brush
- scissors

from one artist to another

BE WATCHING FOR A NEWLY EMERGING STYLE DUBBED "EASTERN ECLECTIC" (OR "ZEN KITSCH"). THIS NEW STYLE CELEBRATES CLASHING COLORS, VINTAGE ASIAN CLUTTER AND A "MORE IS MORE" ATTITUDE VERY UNLIKE PREVIOUS ASIAN-INSPIRED DESIGN STYLES.

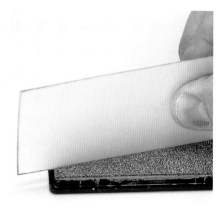

1. **CUT PAPER, PRACTICE STAMPING**
   Cut the white mulberry paper to 9" × 9¼"
   (23cm × 24cm) or to a size that covers the
   entire pillar of the candle up to the bottom of
   the top rim. Practice using the gold inkpad
   and stamp on a scrap of white mulberry paper.
   Place scrap paper under the mulberry paper
   because the ink will bleed through.

2. **STAMP MULBERRY PAPER**
   Using the gold inkpad, the Chinese postage
   stamp and the text stamp with Chinese luck
   symbols, stamp gold images on the piece of
   white mulberry paper. Center both images on
   the paper, placing one higher than and diago-
   nal to the other.

3. **OUTLINE TAG IN GOLD AND STAMP**
   Dip each edge of the vellum tag into the gold
   inkpad to create a border. Apply the "To and
   From" stamp onto the left center of the vellum
   tag using the gold inkpad.

4. **COVER CANDLE WITH GLUE**
   Dip the bristle brush into the water-based
   glue, and cover the glass surface of the candle.
   Before adhering the mulberry paper to the
   candle, locate the side seams in the glass and
   use those as the sides of your project.

5. **ADHERE PAPER TO CANDLE**
   Starting in the center front of the candle,
   position the stamped mulberry paper. Finish
   adhering the paper to the candle. If the seam
   is not glued down securely, add additional glue
   by gently lifting up the seam and adding a little
   extra glue underneath with the bristle brush.

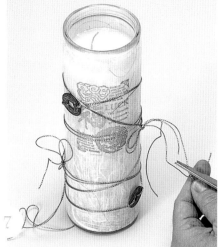
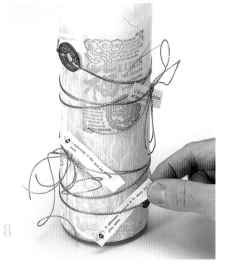

6. **ATTACH COINS TO GOLD THREAD**
Fold two strands of gold thread in half. Attach each doubled gold thread to a Chinese coin with a lark's knot. Repeat with two more strands of gold thread and another coin.

7. **WIND THREAD AROUND CANDLE**
Crisscross the gold threads around the candle so that the coin is in the bottom front and tie the ends in the back or on the side. Repeat with the other Chinese coin and gold thread at the top of the candle. Trim the ends of the thread to a pleasing length.

8. **ADD FORTUNES**
Tuck a few fortunes under the gold thread.

9. **TIE ON TAG AND ADD FINISHING TOUCHES TO CANDLE**
Tie the tag onto the candle with a 2-foot (60cm) length of gold thread around the bottom of the lip of the glass candle. (First tie a knot, then slip the tag on and secure it with a bow.) Using a toothpick, tuck some bits of gold sparkling fiber around the knots in the gold thread, and wrap a bit around the gold thread tied around the top of the candle.

it's a wonderful life

I'M SO BUSY DECORATING PROFESSIONALLY DURING THE CHRISTMAS SEASON THAT IT'S A MIRACLE THAT WE HAVE A TREE IN OUR HOME. A FEW YEARS AGO, RATHER THAN CLAMORING FOR STOWED-AWAY DÉCOR, I LOOKED AROUND THE HOUSE AND QUICKLY SPOTTED COKE CANS—RED AND SILVER WITH SANTA ON THEM—PERFECT! IT WOULD BE AN "IT'S A WONDERFUL LIFE" CINEMA TREE. THE TREE WAS COMPLETE WITH OLD MOVIE TICKET STUBS TUCKED INTO THE BRANCHES. GARLANDS WERE MADE TO LOOK LIKE FILM WITH TITLES PRINTED ON ADDING MACHINE TAPE. I ADDED RED AND WHITE STRIPED POPCORN BAGS FILLED WITH GOODIES, WIDE RED AND SILVER WIRED RIBBON, CELLOPHANE WRAPPED POPCORN BALLS SAYING "ACT III" (LUCKY FIND!) AND A FEW OTHER SUPPORTING ELEMENTS. OH YES, THE COKE CANS WERE HUNG BY THE CHIMNEY WITH CARE—WITH SILVER CORDING! IT WAS A TOTALLY SPONTANEOUS, LIGHTHEARTED NOD TO "POP CULTURE." THINK OUTSIDE THE CAN!

zen
wall treatment

environment in viro (n)·mənt *n* the circumstances, objects, or conditions by which one is surrounded

This technique can be used on an entire wall, or you can make it a movable feast and apply it to canvas. Whatever image you choose, remember to consider the size of the area to be covered. If images are too small, the image will be virtually lost and you will just see spots of color. Be careful when you plan out your random look—it often requires forethought and isn't random at all in application. You don't have to stop with walls—adding these decorative papers onto unlikely surfaces such as chairs and small wall focal points is easily done as well. Applying papers to furniture creates environments of intriguing individuality. For example, my piano has European images découpaged over a large percentage of its surface. To match, the flat rungs on a ladder-back chair are done as well.

MATERIALS AND TOOLS

- 16" × 20" (41cm × 51cm) ready-made pre-primed canvas (Fredrix)
- images from napkin with roses, red poppies or Asian characters
- 1 to 2 oz. beeswax
- joint compound, 1 to 2 cups
- antiquing medium (Apple Butter Brown by Plaid)
- water-based glue, thinned
- electric gluepot
- old butter knife
- foam brush
- bristle brush (for wax)
- rag or paper towel

from one artist to another

WHEN LAYERING WAX, STAIN AND JOINT COMPOUND, ALLOW EACH ELEMENT TO DRY BEFORE CONTINUING. TO ACHIEVE THE DESIRED EFFECT, YOU CAN CONTINUE LAYERING EACH ELEMENT MULTIPLE TIMES. LAYERS ADD MORE DIMENSION AND RICHER NUANCES OF COLOR AND TEXTURE, THOUGH IF YOU ADD TOO MANY LAYERS, YOU MAY CREATE A SURFACE THAT IS TOO MUDDY OR BUSY—ALWAYS SEEK THE RIGHT BALANCE.

1. **ADHERE ROSE IMAGES**
    Découpage the torn napkin images onto the canvas (or wall), creating some distance between them, moving from left to right and from top to bottom. The placement should be random so that there is no noticeable pattern. Also, make sure to leave nice margins at the edges of images, and, if applying to a wall, leave margins at adjacent walls as well.

2. **APPLY JOINT COMPOUND**
    Use the butter knife to apply joint compound around the images. Smooth the plaster down by dragging the knife in random directions over the top.

3. **APPLY ANTIQUING MEDIUM**
    Using the foam brush, apply antiquing medium to a few random areas around the images. Rub the medium in well with a rag or paper towel.

handy tip

THIS PROJECT IS NOT FOR APPLICATION TO WALLS THAT WILL RECEIVE DIRECT SUNLIGHT OR IN A ROOM THAT HEATS UP CONSIDERABLY BEYOND WHAT IS CONVENTIONALLY COMFORTABLE FOR HUMAN BEINGS. THE WAX USED WILL BEGIN TO MELT IF HEATED BEYOND A CERTAIN TEMPER-ATURE (195°F).

4. **APPLY WAX TO CANVAS**

Heat the wax in the gluepot to 190°F to 195°F (wax will boil at 200°F). Apply the wax with a bristle brush using a back-and-forth, vertical and horizontal cross-hatch motion. Apply an even, thin layer of wax to the images to protect them from the antiquing medium. Leave some open spaces, but apply the wax to the majority of the canvas.

5. **APPLY MORE ANTIQUING MEDIUM**

Using the foam brush, apply more antiquing medium over the wax using the same technique as before. Avoiding the central points of the images, bleed the antiquing medium into the sides of the images and apply it in various random spots on the canvas (or wall) to create balance.

6. **APPLY MORE JOINT COMPOUND**

Apply joint compound to create a balanced randomness that builds interest and variation, using the same technique as before. Feel free to use your hands to create different textures. If you choose to work on a canvas, plaster and stain the sides of the canvas so you won't need a frame. You could also experiment by adding red paint (or any other color) around the edges as an accent. Allow the plaster to dry. Repeat layering the wax, stain and joint compound until the desired effect is achieved.

Italianate Wall Technique

Using a different paper gives this wall technique a completely different feel. For this variation, I've used a paper that creates an Italianate feel with its architectural swirls. (Paper napkins used are Sansoucci from Ideal Home Range.)

shadow box

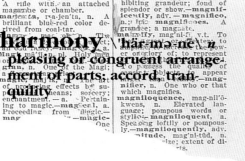

Papers with small prints are particularly suitable for this diminutive design that couples Asian influences with an informal Western sensibility. The mother-of-pearl buttons were impossible to resist, given their association with ancient Asian history and the replicated flower shape on the paper. Natural waxed string repeats the wood tone, continuing the relaxed and harmonious feel of the piece. Finally, adding rhinestones and glitter is a simple way to give this piece a lighthearted aspect and extra dimension. Since this design is meant to be soothing and refreshing, be sure to choose paper with a style that isn't too busy or high contrast. If you choose to paint the shadow box, light mulberry paper will stand out well against a dark background.

MATERIALS AND TOOLS

- 8" × 8" (20cm × 20cm) natural wood shadow box (Walnut Hollow)
- scrapbook paper cut to size 6¹⁄₁₆" × 6¹⁄₁₆" (15cm × 15cm)
- 4 chopsticks
- waxed string
- white mulberry paper
- rice
- Asian character stamps (Joy, Fortunate, Friend)
- black inkpad
- blue rhinestones
- mother-of-pearl daisy-shaped beads
- iridescent blue beads
- blue stardust glitter
- Magical Multi-Color glitter spray (Krylon)
- spray adhesive (Super 77 by 3M)
- hot glue gun and glue sticks
- tacky glue (Aleene's Quick Dry Tacky Glue)

from one artist to another

ORIGAMI PAPERS COME IN 6" × 6" (15CM × 15CM) SIZE AND WORK WELL FOR THIS PROJECT. THEY LEAVE A SMALL INTERIOR BORDER OF NATURAL WOOD THAT COMPLEMENTS THE DESIGN.

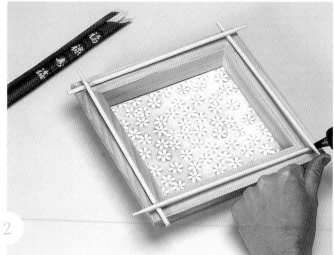

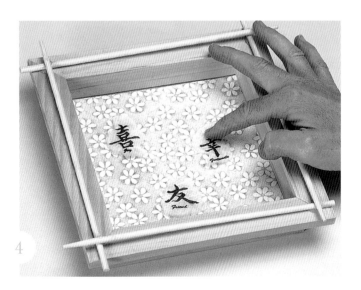

1. **ADHERE PAPER TO BOX BOTTOM**
Cut a piece of scrapbook paper to a size that
fits the bottom of the shadow box (about 6⅛"
[15cm] square). Spray the back of the paper
square with Super 77 and stick it to the bottom
of the shadow box.

2. **GLUE DOWN CHOPSTICKS**
Position three chopsticks, one on each of
three adjacent shadow box ledges, so that each
one overlaps the next. Lift up one end of the
first chopstick and place a dot of glue underneath it. Adhere that end of the first chopstick. The first chopstick will be resting on the
second chopstick, so place a drop of glue
under that end of the second chopstick and
adhere it to the box. Then glue the unglued
end of the first chopstick to the top of the second chopstick. Continue to overlap the chopsticks in this manner until all four are adhered
to the ledge.

3. **CREATE DIMENSIONAL ELEMENTS**
Stamp the Asian character stamps onto the
white mulberry paper and rip out the images.
Glue three to four pieces of rice to the back of
each torn-out image with the tacky glue.

4. **ADHERE TORN IMAGES TO BOX**
Adhere the torn stamped images to the paper
background in the shadow box by putting tacky
glue on the pieces of rice. Arrange them in a
pleasing order, leaving irregular margins
around each one.

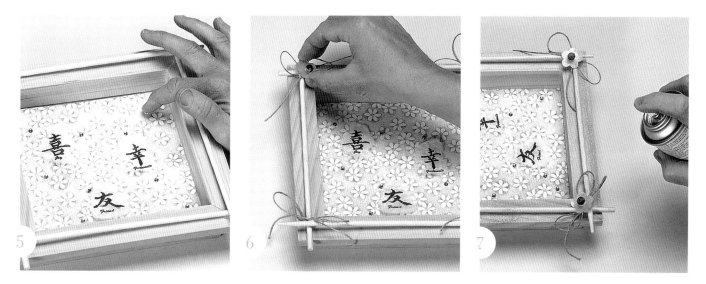

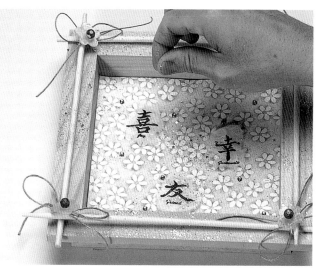

5. **ADD BLUE RHINESTONES**
Using tacky glue, adhere about ten blue rhinestones to the paper on the bottom of the shadow box, orienting them around the torn stamped images.

6. **ADD WAXED-STRING BOWS WITH BEADS AND DAISIES**
Hot glue a blue bead to the center of a mother-of-pearl flower. Repeat for three other blue beads and mother-of-pearl flowers. Cut four 20" (57cm) lengths of waxed string and tie each one in a knot and then in a bow. Glue one bow onto each corner with tacky glue and trim the ends. Then glue a mother-of-pearl and blue bead combination on top of each bow. As you place the bead combinations, tip the flowers in toward the center of the box.

7. **SPRAY ON GLITTER**
Spray the edges of the shadow box with the Magical Multi-Color glitter spray. Some glitter will fall into the center, but avoid spraying excessive glitter directly onto the center.

8. **SPRINKLE STARDUST GLITTER**
While the glitter spray is still wet, sprinkle the stardust glitter on top of it so that it will stick. Lightly sprinkle the glitter around the three stamped images and in other random spots on the frame.

hang a blessing

THE DIMINUTIVE SIZE OF THIS ACCESSORY REQUIRES PROPER PLACING SO THAT IT IS NOT OVERWHELMED BY OTHER DECORATIVE ELEMENTS. YOU MIGHT HANG IT SOMEWHAT LOW ON A WALL, PERHAPS NEAR A LAMP AND CONVERSATION AREA. OR HANG IT ABOVE THE NIGHTSTAND IN A SPARE BEDROOM AND YOUR GUEST, A DEPENDENT TRAVELER, WILL FEEL QUITE ENDEARED WHEN NOTICING THE PIECE PLACED WITH CARE BY THE BED. VIEWED JUST BEFORE RETIRING, IT'S THE LAST SENTIMENT OF KINDNESS BESTOWED BY THE HOST, REASSURING THE WEARY TRAVELER WITH THOUGHTS OF WELCOME AND THANKFULNESS JUST BEFORE SLUMBER.

The office or dignity of a magistrate; the body of magistrates...

Magnolia.

magnolia, mag-...

121

scented
sand bowl

balance \ba-lən(t)s\ *v.t.*
to bring into harmony or proportion

In this project, an unlikely home hardware item is transformed into a peaceful work of art. By adhering some grass-motif paper and ribbon to this metal reducer, and by adding a few soft touches like the tags, metal spirals and scented sand, a utilitarian object finds artful purpose. I love the way the natural wood tone contrasts with the tin. Notice also how the thin, straight lines of the crisscrossing skewers contrast with the round, metal shape of the reducer. And placing the skewers in a somewhat random pattern across the sand lets the fragrance come out and provides a barrier for errant kitties! But kitties aren't the only ones unable to resist playing in the sand. I've had scented sand displayed in various business locations and have enjoyed watching the irresistible desire people have to make impressions in it.

MATERIALS AND TOOLS

- metal reducer (part of a stovepipe), 6" × 8" (15cm × 25cm)
- sand-blasting sand (about 4 cups)
- fragrance oil (orange blossom, water lilies or jasmine work well, or choose your own)
- orrisroot granules
- inexpensive plate or bowl (to create false bottom)
- green scrapbook paper (grid pattern)
- 3½ yards (3m) narrow ribbon (⅜" [1cm]) to coordinate with paper
- 5 circular tags with metal rim (must accommodate stamp size with margin)
- floral stamp
- black inkpad

- metal spirals (or 16- or 18-gauge wire to make your own)
- 5 buttons with shank
- shishkabob skewers (bamboo)
- water-based glue, slightly thinned
- medicine dropper
- vinegar and rag
- Goof Off (optional, for removing labels)
- hot glue gun and glue sticks
- bristle brush
- needle-nose pliers
- nippers
- scissors
- paper towel

from one artist to another

ANOTHER IDEA FOR EMBELLISHING THE TOP OF THE SAND BOWL IS TO DECORATE THE TOP WITH BUTTONS AND EXTRA SPIRAL CLIPS OR EVEN CORDING. YOU CAN ALSO DRAW A SPIRAL WITH A PENCIL, STARTING FROM THE CENTER AND MOVING OUT TOWARD THE EDGE, CREATING A CLEAN SPIRAL-CUT LINE IN THE SAND. YOU COULD EVEN PROVIDE A DRAWING IMPLEMENT, SUCH AS A SMOOTH TWIG, NEXT TO THE SAND BOWL AND ENCOURAGE GUESTS TO MAKE THEIR OWN DESIGNS IN THE SAND.

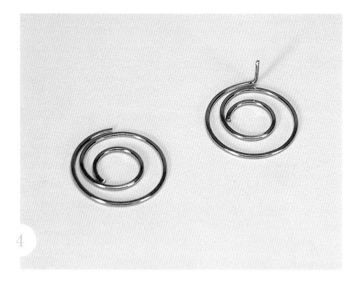

1. **ADHERE PAPER TO BASE**
   Clean the metal reducer with vinegar and a rag. Cut two 1⅜"- (3cm) wide pieces of green paper to fit around the base of the metal reducer when placed end to end, overlapping slightly (about 20½" [52cm]). Dip the bristle brush into the thinned water-based glue (four parts glue to one part water), and brush it onto the base of the metal reducer. Adhere the strips of green paper and secure the ends.

2. **TIE RIBBON OVER PAPER STRIP**
   Take a slightly moistened piece of paper towel and wipe off any excess glue. Wrap a piece of the narrow ribbon around the green paper and tie it in a knot in the back, over the seam.

3. **STAMP CIRCLE TAGS**
   Turn all the tags to the same side. (The metal rims are slightly wider on the front.) Remove the string. Use black ink to stamp the center of each tag with the flower stamp.

4. **BEND UP SPIRAL ENDS**
   Grab the end of a spiral (¼" [13mm] from the end) with the needle-nose pliers and roll your wrist to bend up the wire at a 90-degree angle. Repeat for the remaining spirals, and trim the prongs uniformly.

5. **SATURATE ORRISROOT WITH SCENT**
   Pour a small handful (about ½ cup) of orrisroot into a plastic bag containing about four cups of sand, allowing it to rest on top of the sand. Fill a medicine dropper with your desired fragrance and saturate the orrisroot with about four to six droppers full.

6. **MIX ORRISROOT INTO SAND**
When the orrisroot has been completely saturated, mix it into the sand using a spoon or shake the closed bag around carefully.

7. **CREATE FALSE BOTTOM**
Insert a salvaged plate or bowl into the metal reducer and position it down as far as it will go. Run hot glue around the edges of the plate or bowl to secure the false bottom. Make sure to fill any dents in the tin with hot glue.

8. **ATTACH SPIRALS**
Attach the spirals to the top edge of the metal reducer by sliding the inner coil to the inside edge of the tube and keeping the remaining coils on the outside. The bent-up part of the coil should be at the bottom of the spiral, facing in toward the metal reducer. Slide a stamped metal tag onto the prong of the first coil, then slide a button onto the next spiral. Fill each of the spirals. Slide them around to space them evenly, but don't scratch the tin.

9. **TIE ON RIBBON, POUR SAND IN BOWL**
Wrap a piece of ribbon around the top seam on the metal reducer. Tack the ribbon down in the front with a small dot of hot glue and tie it in a knot in the back. Trim the ends of the ribbon. Pour the scented sand into the bowl.

10. **CRISSCROSS SKEWERS OVER SAND**
Agitate the bowl to settle the sand. Position the bamboo skewers by sliding them through the center of a spiral on each side of the bowl to hold them in place. Crisscross the skewers in a random pattern.

Nos. 1 to 15   Nos. 16 to 30   Nos. 31 to 45   Nos. 46 to 60   Nos. 61 to 75

B I N G O

	16		48	
17	44		66
12	29		53	63
10		36	47	71
19	43		

Start with Letter **O** in Center, Free
5 NUMBERS ACROSS ANY LINE WINS
12 DIFFERENT WAYS TO BINGO

3

ONE STAR SERIES   TOTAL SETS 3,000 CARDS   Printed in U.

To one I love

MAKE A COLOR COPY OF THIS PAGE AND USE ANY OF THE IMAGES TO MAKE YOUR OWN
UNIQUE COLLAGE ARTWORK. ALL IMAGES COURTESY OF THE VINTAGE WORKSHOP.

INSPIRING WEBSITES

The Internet is a huge inspirational playground, and I've spent my fair share of time lost in cyberspace looking at amazing things. Below I share with you some of my favorite Internet resources that I visit frequently for supplies, information and inspiration.

WWW.ERNSTSEED.COM

A useful website for finding botanical names for common plants such as *Helianthus*, which is Latin for sunflower. Simply click on the search button, then on the common name index.

WWW.TRANSLATION.LANGENBERG.COM

This is a website where you can translate any English word or phrase into the language of your choice (Latin not available).

WWW.CARTERJUNK.COM

A former top-level executive at Ralph Lauren, Mary Randolph Carter Berg pioneered the concept of junk as chic, and she'll help you embrace your inner junker! She has also produced some fabulous books on collecting junk, which are previewed on her site.

WWW.TRACYPORTER.COM

Tracy Porter and her husband run an internationally known design and licensing firm and work with high-quality manufacturers to produce stylish home goods. I love Tracy's designs, and her entrancing books, too! There is also some excellent information about designing for licensing.

WWW.WHIPPLEART.COM

Lynn Whipple is an established artist who is revered for her talents and sensibility. Her whimsical and quirky "portraits" are absurdly beautiful. She's an artists' artist with a legion of fans and devotees always filled with anticipation for what she will do next. Find out more about her and her work on this website.

WWW.TEESHAMOORE.COM
WWW.THETATTEREDCIRCUS.COM

These sister websites are rich with voluminous, inspiring artwork and tons of great links to other often quirky websites. Both sites are wonderful découpage resources, with many "collage sheets" and rubber stamps for sale at reasonable prices.

WWW.DECORATORSBOUTIQUE.COM/DB_ACCENTS.HTM

This site provides several links with French- and European-inspired home furnishings. Some of the websites are in other languages, but most have an English-language option. You'll learn a lot from the pictures, regardless.

WWW.CRAFTDESIGNERS.ORG

The website for the Society of Craft Designers offers tremendous opportunities for professional designers by acting as a liaison between publishers, editors, manufacturers and the crafter.

WWW.FORGOTTEN-NY.COM

This website is an interesting retro visual smorgasbord, keeping the old stuff alive. It's full of all of the oddities—big and small, past and present—that define New York City. There are lots of imagination triggers to inspire you.

WWW.ART-E-ZINE.CO.UK/ARTELINKS.HTML-

If you can get past the impossible background, you'll see a ton of fabulous links to amazing artists who work in many different medias and create inspiring art.

WWW.ANNBALDWIN.COM

Ann Baldwin, a British transplant now living in San Francisco, is a talented abstract expressionist, or "abstractionist," who incorporates words, letters and various other kinds of texts into her artwork. In her most recent works, she uses melted wax.

WWW.VAMPSTAMPNEWS.COM/LINKS.HTML

This site has lots of links (and diversity) related to rubber stamping, scrapbooking and crafting.

RESOURCES

All of the materials used in the projects in this book can be purchased at your local craft, fabric, hardware, scrapbooking and rubber-stamping stores or at discount department stores. If you are unable to find what you need at a local store, contact the manufacturers listed below for a retailer near you.

BEAD STUDIO
266 E. Main Street, Ashland, OR 97520
(541) 488-3037
www.beadstudio.com
travel, retro and landmark charms; slides; mother-of-pearl flower beads and iridescent blue beads

DIANE D. FLOWERS, MFT ENTERPRISES
2460 Castlemaine Court, Duluth, GA 30097
(678) 779-0733
www.mftenterprises.com
reindeer moss in a variety of colors

DOVER PUBLICATIONS
31 E. 2nd Street, Mineola, NY 11501
(516) 294-7000
www.doverpublications.com
"Old Time Fruits and Flowers Vignettes in Full Color"

DUNCAN ENTERPRISES
5673 E. Shields Ave., Fresno, CA 93727
(800) 438-6226
www.duncancrafts.com
PSX rubber stamps; Tulip-brand chicken rub-ons; and Aleene's Instant Découpage Glue Sealer and Finish and Aleene's Quick Dry Tacky Glue

KRYLON
(800) 4KRYLON
www.krylon.com
Make It Crackle!, Make It Last!, Preserve It! and Make It Acid-Free!; all spray paints and primers

OFF THE STREETS/COLETTE GEORGE DESIGNS
198 Briar Hills Ave., Riddle, Oregon 97469
(541) 874-3246
www.colettedesigns.net
ceramic acorns

PLAID ENTERPRISES PNC. / ALL NIGHT MEDIA
3225 Westech Drive, Norcross, Georgia 30092
(800) 842-4197
www.plaidonline.com
alphabet stamps; scrapbook paper used in Bird Canvas and variation cabinet panel; Mod Podge and Mod Podge Sparkle

ROMANCE RIBBONS & TEXTILES
Portland, Oregon 97225
(800) 998-1790
exquisite ribbons and buttons

SUSAN OSBORNE LICENSING, INC.
PO Box 3285, Walnut Creek, CA 94598
(925) 969-0264
susan@susanosbornelicensing.com
licensing information

TARA MATERIALS
Tara Materials, Inc. Box 646
111 Fredrix Alley, Lawrenceville, GA 30046
www.fredrixartistcanvas.com
(800) 241-8129 ext. 299 for customer service
Fredrix artist canvas by the yard and on stretchers in various sizes, as well as canvas placemats and coasters

TRACY PORTER
www.tracyporter.com
wallpaper, alphabet stickers, scrapbook paper

THE VINTAGE WORKSHOP
PO Box 30237, Kansas City, MO 64112
(913) 648-2700
www.thevintageworkshop.com
downloads & artwork on cd-roms

WALNUT HOLLOW
1409 State Road 23, Dodgeville, WI 53533-2112
(800) 950-5101
www.walnuthollow.com
wood round, slider-top box, shadow box, clock

find creative inspiration and instruction
in other fine NORTH LIGHT BOOKS!

COLLAGE DISCOVERY WORKSHOP: BEYOND THE UNEXPECTED

by Claudine Hellmuth ISBN 1-58180-678-7, paperback, 128 pages, #33267-K
In a follow-up to her first workshop book, Claudine taps into a whole new level of creativity with *Beyond the Unexpected*. Inside you'll find original artwork and inventive ideas that show you how to personalize your own collage pieces using new techniques and interesting surfaces. In addition, the extensive gallery compiled by Claudine and other top collage artists will spark your imagination. Whether you're a beginner or a collage veteran, you'll enjoy this lovely book both as inspiration and as a practical guide.

PAPERCRAFTING ROOM BY ROOM

by Deborah Spofford ISBN 1-58180-656-6, paperback, 128 pages, #33243-K
If you want intriguing paper projects that go beyond just basic cards and gifts, this book is for you. This premier book will show you how to turn ordinary home items into extraordinary, stylish pieces. Inside you'll find projects for crafting accents for every room in the house, including embellishing lampshades, clocks, tabletops and more. You'll love using simple techniques such as découpage to add flourish to gorgeous and functional pieces.

ALTERED BOOKS WORKSHOP

by Bev Brazelton ISBN 1-58180-535-7, paperback, 128 pages, #32889-K
A book isn't just a book anymore—it can have windows, doors, drawers and more. *Altered Books Workshop* gives you comprehensive instruction and inspiration for creating multi-dimensional art that is a reflection of your moods, thoughts and life. You'll learn how to turn old books into dazzling works of art by combining mixed media and papercrafting techniques with elements of collaging, journaling, rubber stamping and scrapbooking. You'll love learning the wide range of creative techniques for crafting unique, personalized altered books offered in the over 50 projects and ideas inside *Altered Books Workshop*.

COLLAGE CREATIONS

by Kim Ballor, Barbara Mathiessen and Tracia Williams ISBN 1-58180-546-2, paperback, 128 pages, #32894-K
Collage Creations is the perfect introduction to the exciting world of collage. In this guide, you'll learn how to use a variety of easy collage techniques to make ordinary items extraordinary. Soon you'll be filling your home with gorgeous personalized artwork. Featuring over 20 step-by-step projects and a section on stress-free design, this book will inspire you to create collages on frames, boxes, journals, tabletops and more!

These books and other fine titles are available from your local art & craft retailer, bookstore, online supplier or by calling 1-800-448-0915.